Quotes
To
Graduate
By

By Forest D. Bynum

To my brother Nicholas and all of those who support me to Study Abroad

Bŷnum
Industries
Inc.

Quotes To Graduate By

words of wisdom for the aspiring college graduate

By Forest D. Bynum

Copyright © 2019 by Forest D. Bynum

Published By Bynum Publishing, a subsidiary or Bynum Industries Inc.

Baton Rouge 2019

ISBN 978-0-578-44427-7

Foreword:

As my tassel flowed on that day of May 12, 1998, I was set on dreams of becoming a Chemical Engineer at LSU. I excelled in the community service arts, academic competitions, and surviving eight siblings in a lower socio-economic environment. I hit the LSU campus with a forgetful summer semester. The fall semester was a huge turning point in my life as I not only learned about who Christ really was, but I accepted him in my life. Church use to be a hinderance in my study schedule as I was dragged into a 45 minutes car ride to Slidell to listen to people I did not know and did not understand why I had to go. I saw my fellow classmates go to football games and fun outings as I was delegated to whatever pastimes on the perimeter of the campus.

My efforts in the classroom were mediocre. I had some B's and C's, but I also failed a few classes that year. There were some health problems, but I found myself out of learning and without direction. I wandered the streets for a few weeks until a friend let me stay permanently. I had trouble finding work. I did a few temp jobs but nothing amounting to the satisfaction that I know now as a hard day's work. At one point, I did not have work for four months and almost lost my place in the corner or the apartment where my bag of clothes lies. I finally settled for a position at a diner where I was subjected to simple but meaningful tasks that would catapult myself to the man I am today.

I started work at Louie's Café working just a few hours during the middle of the night. I learned the mastery of the BBBBLT and the Big Louie. I cleaned floors and bathrooms. I welcomed customers and I was noticed for the first time in my life for working hard instead of being a smart ass. I was blessed with a promotion in three months for my hard work and attention to detail to the dishes going out to the dining room. As my position as shift manager, I learn the basics of accounting, inventory, marketing, management, and networking. I took the challenge to take on responsibility whenever it came. At one point, I was working 72 hours a week and it was tough as I drank way too much Dr. Pepper, but it taught me how much the human body can take. It was stressful as I actually was able to accomplish the feat of falling asleep at a LSU home game where my friends surprised me one weekend after I had worked a double. I eventually was exhausted of my culinary growth and I was tested by an executive chef of another restaurant. I passed the test and was brought in part time where I had to create an original soup before I was an official part of the team. I passed the second test with a Chinese Chicken Noodle Soup. My time at Louie's Café ended, an iconic symbol of Baton Rouge, but I grew as much as I could.

I would always love James Wetherford as he was a great mentor and allowed a nobody to learn the basics of diner cuisine through traditional French cooking techniques. To learn how to sauté, fry, boil, and bake in a high pace setting transformed me from a basic line cook to a chef. He helped me understood the foundation needed for my next endeavor. I worked with Todd Barrios for 18 months and he took me to a new level by introducing me to international ingredients and new techniques. I was able to allow my creativity to soar. I decided to take a chance into the management realm again and I stayed around food service till 2005. I fell into some tough times as I took jobs that no longer allowed me to be creative. I did not feel that I was working hard, but just letting the days waste by as I saw my friends graduate and move on to bigger goals in life.

I was wasting my time in a black hole which was surrounded by a sugary glazed doughnut. I hated my job at the doughnut shop. I found myself daydreaming for hours as there was no direction and I finally had enough. I took the advice of a friend to go to a temp agency.

I took a test and scored really high. They offered me a job, but it did not start for six weeks. They tested my endurance for working for a warehouse where the job started at four in the morning. It was long hours, but they gave me a recommendation to start my career in healthcare.

I did not understand at the time that the job wanted candidates with a college degree. Apparently, a lot of my fellow co-workers had completed a degree and enjoyed working on the telephone in customer service. I was grateful, and I took for granted at the time that it was an office job. I ate my words very quickly as I entered my first true job training. It was an intense 14 weeks of training. I did not know what Medicare was and I was eager to learn, but it was tough. The company expected a lot, but I was ready for the most part. My first day we were challenged to find a way to help digitize a training manual. So, I went to work and came up with an idea at home and the next day presented to the trainer. She liked my idea and helped implemented it along with helping her in other tasks. I wanted to find a way off the telephone, for I did not necessarily like being on the phone, but it was important for my development as a businessman. I came to find out how stressful work can get. I literally had to stay at my desk for eight hours a day. One call came after another with highly technical questions. It was extremely stressful when Hurricane Katrina hit Baton Rouge. It changed the landscape of how business was done at my job.

Our company was instructed to be a hotline for lost beneficiaries and we would assist them in finding medical services across the US. Evacuees were being sent as far as Salt Lake City without any ID. I remember a couple of things from the hurricane. I was blessed because the only material thing I lost was a half of grapefruit I left in my apartment. My apartment lost power for a week, but a friend I had just met allowed us to stay at her place. I also helped the company by training a team of reps to do written correspondence to assist in the inquires of the lost beneficiaries. The most memorable thing was when my dear friend Deanne challenged me to do something I never had done before to relieve my stress. I told of the story that I would read books of different countries when I was real young, and I always wanted to go to Spain. I told no one else and bought my ticket to Madrid that night. This would be the start of the rekindling of my love of Latin America. I had done mission work in Mexico for four years but traveling on my own I could really sink into the language and culture.

I learned so much about how the government operates and healthcare in general. I develop my skills as an administrator. I had health insurance for the first time. I learned about saving money as this was the first time I has disposable income. The exposure to travel helped me create a budget so I could continue to travel. I was able to go to the ends of the Earth in Ushuaia, Argentina. I learned about other languages as I spent six weeks in Brazil and learned the basics of Portuguese. I studied for a year and traveled to Catalonia to put into practice my Catalan. This also was the time I started dating and learned that I really hated dating because most women were only looking for money or sex. Eventually I maximized my potential in healthcare administration. I was a supervisor of a Medicaid contract and I could not get compensated for my work as I should. Turns out a college degree would have helped but I took the chance and looked for another job that would treat me with the respect that I should have received and the money I deserved for my leadership and perseverance in the healthcare arena.

I spent ten months looking for work. While looking for work, I published my first book, a cookbook on Latin America called the Delicious Commission. I wanted to make sure I could publish it as I wanted to leave a legacy for my grandchildren. Things looked bleak as I took a wrong foray into the financial sector by getting a worthless certification that brought me no additional money and a dead-end temp job. It was August of 2012 and I was penniless and despite interviews, I could not find work. I wound up in the hospital after I had thoughts of suicide and afterwards found solace in a church building.

It was a tumultuous time in the building as it had huge holes in the ceiling and it was infested with roaches and rats. It took a couple of months to clean the place up where it was a respectable place to lay one's head. I continued my job search for another 24 months as I was exposed to a different part of Baton Rouge. As the rest of the barrios in my city, it needed Jesus, but it was to be approached in a different way. To pass the time away, I had to trick myself that I was speaking with people as I only saw the church folk on Sunday and on an occasional weekend where a band would play melodious tunes of rhythm and blues. I knew deep down that some of these folks were instruments of the gospel, but I did not feel fulfilled on a spiritual level. I would listen to hours of podcast. I was constantly writing new ideas and would steal money from the change jar to buy cups of delicious CC's coffee to keep my sanity and I wanted to feel like a regular person. Even though I had over 40 interviews during this time, I still could not find work. I published two more books during this period. I also stared at the blank white walls. I watched endless hours of basketball and sumo clips. I thought to myself many of times if this was the life I would live forever.

I was finally able to get full time work in December 2014 as a Medical Records Supervisor. I worked through the holidays to get the company back to working order. I wrote a training manual and started an auditing procedure. I finally found a way to get back into the way of the hardworking man. I learned very quickly on this job that nothing is guaranteed. I received a pink slip six months into the job as my job was just contracted for this work. I took one of the biggest gambles of my life. I accepted a lateral position for the company I contracted for and bought a ticket to back to Spain, my patria culiniara. It was a great ten days and I was challenged by a friend to try to find work that I loved to do. I always wanted to travel for work overseas, so I completed an ESL certification when I came back from Seville. It was easy, too easy, apparently you are supposed to do it over a few months. I got an A and did it in two weeks. Then I started to look for work and every company not only wanted me to pay to teach, but they also wanted a college degree. I was devastated but determined to continue my professional career.

I worked for the next year helping to prepare appeals for Medicare and complex medical records issues. I enjoyed my teammates especially the nurses I worked with. I loved those ladies, but my reputation preceded me. I was made fun of in every way. They did not like my lifestyle as I still stayed in the sanctuary of the church due to the laws of eviction. I still rode the bus and did not wear designer clothes. I was even made fun of my hair. My issue was the management never complained. I made to work every day on time. I always completed my work. I was available for any special projects, but it wasn't enough. I was fired for making an alleged loud noise. I did not receive any support from my church when I was fired, so I decided based on my previous life experiences, I needed one last adventure, for I did not know when I would be able to go again. I left for Nicaragua for more learning of the Spanish language.

I originally decided to go for two weeks but changed to a month after recalculating my budget. I saw a different side of Nicaragua. One different of the media portrayal of violence and corruption. I saw adventure, kind people, lots of fried chicken, and a new window of learning. Despite being followed by the police for my journey because I don't think they understood that I was there to learn and not to cause mischief, I still had a great time. I arrived during the celebrating of the Sandistas and learned about the struggles of the poor and the very poor. I saw it all in color as the marketplaces dictated the state of the nation. Nicaragua does not produce a whole lot of goods and services, but it had a lot of human capital. The nicaragüense were very nice, it was the ex-pats that did not like me around. I found a prejudice because I was an African-American in a predominately upper class white society. I got to hike a volcano, swam in a volcano, went hiking in a canyon, participated in the patron saint festivals, and rode several chicken buses. I did a little writing, but it was hard to focus from the discrimination. I abandoned two projects and this book is the first real attempt back into my professional authoring career.

When I came back from my Central American adventure, I left the church to wander into a squatter's house. It was filthy and broken down. The heater broke as temperatures that winter fell below 15 F. I searched for jobs the next nine months or so before I was told to leave. I managed to call a friend to store my books and clothes and a few precious trinkets. At the last moment I started a temp job as a teacher administrator of a state wide graduate exit tests. I had to use my pay to purchase a hotel to keep my commitment with the school. When I was done with the job, I left the hotel with a suitcase of dress clothes, a backpack of two T-shirts, some basics necessities and a Portuguese book. I left my towel in the hotel…I found out I did not need it on the streets.

I wandered around Baton Rouge that day. It was a Saturday and I tried to not think about my situation. I found myself sleeping under the interstate until someone had reported me to the police. I managed to catch a bus and get to another side of town. I wander to the wee hours of the morning till I found a bench that I would make home. I made a decision back at the squatter house to enroll in college again as a way to find accommodation. It was a risky move, for if someone knew what I was doing, the school may have stopped me from taking courses. I strategically planned hotel stays on my credit card to wash and take care of enrollment and paid my debt to transfer my grades from seventeen years ago to count for classes. I was about maxed out until I made it to three days before school. I just made with enough money to check into the inn three days before school started. I only had enough money to buy a couple of notebooks and a ninety-eight-cent plastic container where I cooked every meal for a month.

The inn was my home for two months. It smelled of despair and hundred-dollar one-night stands. Amidst fights of nonsense and a smoker's paradise, I took twelve hours of college courses including two introductory classes of Spanish, my first accounting class, and a research writing English course. I picked these courses strategically in order to begin my quest of redemption. I needed the accounting and English course to take the other business courses. I chose Spanish because I felt it was my easiest subject and if I was going back, I would take advantage of what college had to offer, knowledge. I learned the Spanish of the calles, now I would get my chance to shine in the classroom.

I would get straight A's and make the Dean's List for the first time in my collegiate career. It was my first A in a college class. My English teacher gave me a 97 on my final paper. I was pleased as I always liked writing especially doing the research. I realized my practice of publishing books really came in handy to organize my ideas and outline the paper. My accounting class was difficult as it was online, and I had to teach myself on the non-reliable Internet access. I was writing a balance sheet and I had to start over on five hours of homework because of the untrustworthiness of the connection at the inn. I came to the conclusion that the 21st century of college classes required steady Internet access. Both of my Spanish classes I received a 98 and it proved all of the traveling around the world showed that administration was my job, but traveling was my university.

From that semester I was able to get Work Study and be employed again. I was able to network an opportunity to volunteer at a church working with a Food Bank to distribute food to the poor. I also was finally able to find my own place to stay. With a new home, I was able to cook my own food, play by my own rules, and write the second chapter of redemption. I declared my major of Business Administration with the hope to return to LSU to complete a degree in International Trade and Finance as my Spanish teacher helped me find online. She encouraged me to do my best and graduate and to continue my learning of the Spanish language.

So, I present to you these messages of encouragement and wisdom. These influential people of history have left a legacy I hope to leave one day. But I chose an array of cast members for this production. It is important that you focus on all aspects of learning, even those outside the classroom. I tried to obtain the widest spectrum of people from many areas of learning. I wanted to show the not so common sayings from these persuasive leaders of their fields.

Also, you will notice my personal contribution to twenty first century philosophy. Throughout my life I have experienced many things that are noteworthy and meaningful. Sometimes my thought s are whimsical but still go into the depths of deep thought that make you look at life through a different lens, even though it may not be rose colored.

I tried not to be biased by the persons overall lifestyle when choosing for the content of this book. Some I agree with their lifestyle and others I don't, but the words that left their lips gave the motivation and desire for the pursuit of academic happiness and the completion of a college degree. These words that are given to you do not replace the sound judgement of wise parents, pastors, youth leaders, school advisors, or the old lady on the block that keeps everyone out of trouble. Consider this book a missing piece of the rompecabezas that I have seemed to ignore for decades. I made many mistakes in my life. Fortunately, none of them have lead to drugs, jail, or unwed pregnancy. I wanted to show you the true advice of a student that has come back for redemption and experiences the same problems and struggles as you complete your program.

"Dr. Pepper invigorate the body, Tea relaxes the mind, but Coffee encapsulates the soul"

- Forest D. Bynum

Date: Jan 12, 2008

Location: National Theater in San Jose, Costa Rica

I always have enjoyed a good beverage whether by myself or with friends. Sometimes caffeinated beverages are needed to stay alert in the college arena. Caffeine and its benefits also comes with precautions. I took some caffeine pills one time and I stayed awake for a week. Caffeine is a drug and you should be careful with your consumption. Water is very important to regulate this use of a stimulant.

However, these drinks are pretty safe in moderation. It was Dr. Pepper that kept me going during my overnight stints at the diner. I had to work 11am to 7am drinking all that high fructose corn syrup. I cut my consumption several years ago, but when I do enjoy a soda, it is delicious. Tea has a unique property of having stimulant and a depressant so it is not as strong. It relaxes me as I day-dream all the time of the camellia plant flowing in the highlands of Darjeeling. However, coffee has really touched my soul.

The best coffee I ever had comes from Costa Rica where its mild climate and hilly terrain allows the arabica bushes to grow the best product of beans in the world. Drinking coffee to me is almost as a religion as following Christ. Trust me on this, sharing a cup of coffee with someone may save your semester.

"A house divided against itself cannot stand."

- Abraham Lincoln

Date: June 16, 1858

Location: Springfield, Illinois

      Luke 11:17 gave Abraham Lincoln the inspiration to best express the pulse of the nation. Are you a free state or a slave state was the prevailing question that informed voters were trying to answer? As college students, we make decisions to voice our opinion. You will learn that by making informed decisions based on facts will show validity in your responses in and out the classroom. You all will be stretch to state your opinion, but always base it on the facts.

      I also am an advocate of being involved in the political process. This is a right that many people fought and died over so that you have the power of who write your laws and governs the state of society. Do not get in the habit of protesting and expressing you right to vote if you are a US citizen and not vote. Believe it or not, there are still countries that do not give this right to its people.

      As being an ambassador of the gospel of Christ Jesus, I also take this verse as it was spoken from the LORD. You can't love Christ and something else. I was told by a former pastor of mine that Jesus plus something is actually taking less of Jesus. So if you follow Christ and go to the temple of the gridiron on Saturdays but do not go to church on Sundays, you lose part of the experience that is the glorious walk with Christ. Death Valley is an amazing experience, but make sure you score touchdowns at your local church.

"Speak softly but carry a big stick "

- Theodore Roosevelt

Date: Sept 2, 1901

Location: Minnesota State Fair

Roosevelt said this in his speeches encouraging the nation that we should be involved in world affairs only when it affects our way of life. The ancient Chinese civilizations also had the same sentiment called xenophobia. The Chinese were afraid of foreign influence to change their way of life. However I say that he was open to ideas but not necessarily always to solve other people's affairs with war. War is expensive and good things can come out of war but at what cost? Human life is precious and his speeches were persuading the people to focus on American production, a long lost art as we have been the founders of the Information Age.

This also brings another valuable lesson that I had to learn the hard way. My friends would get picked on in college by adults and I overacted a few times but I wanted those people to know that my friends are worth fighting for but not actually start an actual fist fight. Conflict resolution is something that you will need to maintain as teachers demand composure in and out the classroom . With the influence of alcoholic beverages on college campuses, temper flair quickly and sometimes over nonsense. I have had to learn to speak only when I can back it up with verifiable truth and sometimes it is better to not say anything at all…just let a nigga sleep.

"Those who cannot remember the past are condemned to repeat it."

- George Santayana

Date: December 16, 1863 – September 26,1952

Location: Unknown

This philosophy professor from Harvard University originally from Spain is said to be the originator of this quote but many varieties of this message exists. Even though I am a business major, history is still is important. If I make too many of a product and have to throw them away, I will remember for the next time to produce less. The same is in history when you make mistakes, remember and learn from them.

On an aggregate scale, this applies to governments and wars that should be started. I am not anti war, but ideological affairs should be dealt with people and not governments by weapons of mass destruction. So by learning history of all people, you can make sound decisions as you will become the future leaders of the world. Don't make a rash decision because you forget to do the research.

When I first was in college, I was offered a credit card and I was hesitant to use until I realized that I had to buy textbooks with no money. I did not have the resources to be successful in college. It showed as I walked away after one year. It took me 16 years to even try to use a credit card again. This time I did my research as I found a secure credit card which had a safety net that I placed a down payment in case I could not pay the bill. I recommend the Discover secure card because they not only gave me back my down payment, but also treated me really nice every time I talked with them. Dealing with good finances will get you one step closer to getting that degree.

"A penny saved is two pence clear "

- Benjamin Franklin

Date: 1737

Location: Poor Richard's Almanac

      Even at the young age as most college students enter maturity, we must learn to save for the future. Investing rather than wasting our daily wages helps us to survive in a world where money only holds its value by the belief in the nation or entity that prints it to be used as currency. This is the real quote that most people do not use when they say a penny saved is a penny earned. This quote is much better because it states the political temperature at the time. Benjamin Franklin is making fun of the British economy saying that colony currency is twice as valuable as the British pound which they were a leading world power at the time. So knowing that investing money can earn interest, it may be t your benefit to save money if mot to make more money, but to make sound investments into your future like I did with traveling.

      I recently learned about current and future consumption by a great professor in aggregate economics. I knew saving is crucial for a great future to not only hard times but for investment. I learned that both values affect the overall output of a nation. Some nations spend so much on human capital, infrastructure, and technology; they forget that the people can make their own decisions about investing in their future.

"There is nothing impossible to him who will try."

- Alexander the Great

Date: 356 BC - 323 BC

Location: Unknown

I understood by my collegiate classes that being smart is not enough. Alexander the Great pushed the limits of exploration and found out by allowing the conquered peoples to practice their own customs and taking the best parts to the other parts of his empire, made him very wise and prosperous. That is why I try to do my best in every paper, project, and class attendance. Show your professors what you learned from them but also outside of academia. It will make you a well-rounded person and a full life.

To do this you must understand that it takes hard work as well as working efficiently. Effort is something that is not normally taught in the classroom, but even geniuses have to keep working hard no matter the subject. You can try many times but if you do not understand; you may need to step back, regain your composure, and then approach it another way. I used this approach for my ECON class in money and banking till I figured out how to interpret the graphs discussed in class. Just like Alexander the

Great, I use different ways to handle all aspects of life and the best ones I keep. To conquer the college life, you will always need to do you best.

" If I reach for the stars and try to lasso the moon but only land in South America, I still have lived an adventurous life. "

- Forest D. Bynum

Date: December 2006

Location: Baton Rouge. Louisiana

After my seventh trip overseas, I realized that my diagnosis of the travel bug was an onset illness. I understood it took me every last cent I had as I overdrawn my bank account after the unexpected emergency of my luggage being sent to Milwaukee but an error of Air Tran airlines. It was worth every dollar of interest I had to pay my bank to get my account in the black again. It would be nice to accomplish the impossible but I realized that goal setting is an important thing in life as well as for the collegian.

I actually completed my mission as I was able to speak at a youth conference in Argentina. I got to share the gospel. I was not trained by a church. Money was not raised to send me. I just met a fellow brother and he asked me to talk to his congregation. I lassoed more than the moon on that day because I truly learned about the word esperanza.

Hope was crucial in my life as being able to travel gave me hope that there was purpose in my life.

La Iglesia de Esperanza was hope for a really poor area called the vicha. It is like the favelas in Brazil. It was a beacon because it had running water and electricity which the members of the church did not have at home. It was truly hope to them. Their goals were simple, to be able to live another day. I am so blessed. Shoot for the moon when you plan you college lifespan, but be satisfied with completion and getting to see something spectacular like South America.

"Don't be a stranger"

— James Wetherford

Date: July 2001

Location: Louie's Cafe

When I left Louie's Café for more advanced training in the culinary arts, I made a mistake. Despite the breakup, he was a great man. He gave me a chance so that I would not become homeless yet again. He even gave me time off to do international mission work. He was a fair man and I kick myself in the head to this day because I realize I do cut off people from my life.

In your dealings in life, you will never know when you need to rely on another person for a reference, a ride, a body part, or just a friend. I am working on that myself to make sound judgements when I no longer associate with a person and when I should keep their business card. As a student, I would advise to make your circle of friends those that not only have similar beliefs but actually try to get good grades. You will have some friends that do not perform as well. To be successful, you need to surround yourself with those who carry the same weight. Notice I did not say anything about socio-economic situation.

Being rich or poor is not an indicator of future success. By not being rich myself, I could understand better those who do not have a lot, but those who do have money usually know how to spend it and more importantly, how to save money. My friend base is a rich background of individuals who have at least one degree. I am the exception as I do not have a degree yet but they accept me as their own. Do not pass up a great friendship because they look snobby or they dress shabby. Find out more than skin deep and invest in them, they could become the highest profit margin in your portfolio of life.

"Try everything at least once"

— Todd Barrios

Date: August 2001

Location: The Kitchen of University Club

How does shark taste? It really does not have bite unless you put a spicy sauce on top. I learned these things as the Executive Chef made me taste everything under the sun. I have tried beef tartare to miso to a variety of demiglace sauces. He exposed me to international cuisine and I was no longer afraid of experimentation with cooking. He gave me the license to drive my creativity into hyperspace to discover new ground in my life.

With tasting new things, you still have to be careful. You have to make sure the food is fresh and not spoiled. If it too spicy or if you have an allergen, you should be extra careful in what you consume. College is like a fusion restaurant with a huge menu. You should walk away with having experiencing lots of new things, but with caution. Fusion can easily can become confusion in a dish when trying to blend two things into one.

When you take this advice, remember everything is not for consumption. Just because it is there, you should not try it. Some things I advocate against are drug use and cult religions that take advantage of young minds. You should dare to find your true self, but not at the expense of your education or your life. There are dangers that exist on campus that stupid people will try to influence you for sex, power, or money. But it should not deter to learn new things and try out ethnic food around your campus, it is pretty tasty.

"Soldiers win battles on the field, Generals win wars in the tents"

– paraphrased by Sun Tsu of The Art of War

Date: 8th century BC - 5th century BC

Location: Ancient China

As a college student, we all have battles. As good soldiers we know that staying organized and being attentive in class, we can win these battle called assignments. It is not war with the professors but a battle in ourselves to train us to be better people and enriched by the knowledge we discover in these sacred halls of higher education.

I learned to be a leader, you have to think long term. Sometimes you have to be a solider but it is the generals that get good grades. My faith in Christ has humbled me to serve him my master and I do little things to make big impact for the Gospel by getting good grades. I challenge every student to get at least a 3.0 every semester. Put yourself in the upper echelon of your field and watch how easy to get an invite to the general's tent.

But to do long term goals, or metas as I learn in my Intermediate Oral Communication class, you have to have CEO Mentality. Think like a business leader when it comes to your classwork. Whether you are on scholarship or waiting tables to take that writing course, you invest money into college and you should treat it as such. When you are done, you will thank me and I challenge you to write thank you cards to those that contributed to you success of your degree. Win the war...graduate...I am still in the trenches with you.

"All of our kids can't aspire to be like Lil Wayne"

– Barack Obama

Date: Jul 16, 2009

Location: 100 year anniversary speech for the NAACP

      I have been known to spit that hot fire amongst good friends every once in a while, but the life of the rapper is a lot more complicated as it is 10% lyrics and 90% image. Hip-hop is more marketing than creative writing. Believe it or not, most professional hip hop artist pay writers to help cultivate their catalogs. Going to college is a great alternative to risking everything into an artform that just became mainstream ten years ago. It is sometimes a good thing to go against the grain, but most of us are just not that talented. School is a good way to earn a living and to learn about life.

      Reciting from the 21st century philosopher Lil Wayne's "Hustler Musik"; "It's not what you walk away from, its what you walk away with." Just because you do not make millions of dollars does not prove your life to be a failure. Most people get unfocused when there primary focus is money. You should not be in college just to get money. You should love what you do like the best hip hop artists do. They work extremely hard to keep up with current events and the beat of society. The musicians understand the influence they have on a generation and beyond. Even the hardest of rappers have come to con-clusions of conservative means. Take Ice T who actually made a song about his dislike for cops when he was young and later became an actor in a show where cops are the protagonist. I have always imagined if I could be a professional basketball player or a rapper. Those who work the hardest can be, but I realized my best work in in business.

"Teamwork is not an occasional act but a permanent attitude"

 - Forest D. Bynum

(paraphrased from the great Dr. Martin Luther King.)

Date: February 2003

Location: Metairie, Louisiana

I learned when I worked at Krispy Kreme, to create a great experience with an established great product, you need everyone to work together. This is a great principle for all majors but especially those in entrepreneurship or business. I did not like working there because I did not get a chance to learn the production line. I wasted away two years of my life. This was the one thing I learned from the experience where if we worked together, things went relativity smooth. When people were battling for money, things went south.

You are going to find out that in a lot of your classes, you will have to do group assignments. You may be paired up with some of the most unsavory people you have met, but like in business, you will have to deal with them in order to get a good grade. To combat this, I will use a technique I learned in my Marketing class. Learn the people's name who sit beside and around you. Get their information the first day of class. You will typically find that people who are willing to share sensitive information can be dealt with in a project setting. Just be careful as some people will want your information to ask you on a date or for cheap sex.

Make sure that your attitude towards the group is positive but reasonable, Be ready to sacrifice time and resources especially if the assignment is a considerable amount of your grade. Make sure you can state to your professor a part that you lead or did by yourself as some of your teammates will throw you under the bus and claim the works as a group effort. Very rarely the work is done as a group but parts of a whole that comes together at the end. If it looks like your team is not willing to give their best, speak with your professor early for advice and you may just have to stick it out, and study harder on the final to recover. I have never heard of a group final to date, but weirder things have happened before.

"If I have seen further than others, it is by standing upon the shoulders of giants"

- Isaac Newton

Date: January 4, 1643 - March 31, 1727

Location: Unknown

Research is developed by learning from past researchers. By doing my own research I have learned giving credit to those that make new discoveries is important. From the predecessors of mathematics, Isaac Newton help discover Calculus which is a game changer in the university arena. He used it to prove his scientific and economic principles. You will discover that most majors that require any research will make you take one Calculus course. Be ready for your mind to be stretched beyond your imagination. You will realize your intro calculus class is just a taste of what he developed on his own.

Most universities and colleges have academic integrity policies. You should always write down the source of your work if you did not come up with it originally, even if you do not turn it in. When you start to receive those high marks and that your professors have access to programs that can show if you plagiarize text, you will thank me later. Learn how to cite your sources and always quote a source if you use more than a few words from its publication. Be mindful of the formatting as they will take off points for that type of silliness.

By taking the time to write in your own words and learn from your past ancestors in your field, you can break new ground and become a giant yourself. You will be required to in most graduate programs. Students in the future will quote you as a source of credible information. Who knows what greatness you can achieve? You may develop a formula or a constant or even a new process or technique. New ideas gives you honor, the university prestige, and even perhaps both money.

"No one is free who has not obtained the empire of himself. No man is free who cannot command himself."

- Pythagoras

Date: 570 BC - 490 BC

Location: Ancient Greece

You can see he is much more than a man of algebraic and geometric concepts. I have known of his most famous theorem since middle school. But he does more than triangulate data into some atmosphere of academia. He was a man of philosophy and thought learning form the great masters being influenced by Egyptians and Romans and well as the advanced Greek society in which he was a member. I learned about him in a World History project in high school. He knew a lot and he let you knew based on my research. He had a sort of ghetto mentality that resides today in some inner city youth.

This quote tells you of the freedom you have as an American. If you work, you can enjoy this freedom. For too long as I ride the public bus I witness individuals who cant command themselves. It is called lying about their disabilities. Some people give up, even though who attempt college and realize they are not smart. Most cases, they do not want to work hard. Just because you are poor does not mean you have a disadvantage or that society has disabled you from being successful. I have fought and scraped for my whole life and I had to work that much harder for a little success. These people who cheat disability cheat themselves. They tell themselves you can only attain this much in life and no more. By completing your degree, you make yourself immune to this plague in lower economic circles. Doors open instead of being kicked down. My foot hurts.

That is why I went back. Redemption of completing my degree is freedom. Yes, I have the freedom to vote, to own land, to travel the seven seas. But I have also been labeled as lazy, slow, and disabled. Those people will never take my freedom. This degree will become the passport of my success.

"When you can do common things of life in an uncommon way, you will command the attention of the world."

- George Washington Carver

Date: January 1, 1864 - January 5, 1963
Location: at Tuskegee University

Mr. Carver was a botanist and an inventor that produced dozens of inventions and processes about simple things to make agriculture a little better. He has completed tremendous work in research and used common means to come to his conclusions. Despite being influenced by the razor sharp rules known as Jim Crow, he managed to excel in an academic environment and contributed to society better methods of growing cotton and many other plants.

I was inspired to start writing by my friend Alledria. She told me that I should put my recipes in a cookbook. It inspired me to write my first book, The Delicious Commission. To me, I am just an ordinary man that Christ allows to do extraordinary things. Imagine that a scientist and an education leader should be remembered more than by processing a peanut into a sandwich spread? Sometimes just looking at ordinary items in a different way can change the world. You will see in college, most schoolwork can be solved by simple means but taking different approaches can allow you to understand your craft a little better. Remember to think simple when trying to complete all the tasks in your daily life. Sometimes you need an uncommon approach in order to see results, because college always has unexpected hurdles that you may need to push over instead of make that leap you are not fit enough to soar over.

"The idea is not to block every shot. The idea is to make your opponent believe that you might block every shot "

- Bill Russell

Date: Feb 12, 1934 - Present

Location: Player/Player Coach of the Boston Celtics

Perception is reality. I love basketball and people do not really understand the impact of the greatest champion in professional sports. I love the fact that in a pair of Chuck Taylors' (I use to have a pair before I was homeless) which have no support, he could score 40 points a night but rather score 18 and defeat such greats as Oscar Robertson and Wilt Chamberlin by playing great defense. His blocks are amazing as I have seen the footage of his blocks being times so perfectly he could rebound the ball and initiate the offense. 3-time defensive Player of the Year Dwight Howard also uses the same techniques to continue to be the behemoth of defense he is today. This is a really good marketing tool, if you can convince people it is a good product, it will sell.

In college, you will need to learn how to market yourself in order to get opportunities to succeed in life and to complete your degree. Sometimes you do not know how to do something but you are willing to learn and take chances and experiment. Bill Russell knew he would not be able to block every shot in a game, but he knew how the game worked. When you understand the mechanics of college and it is just as important to locate the correct resources and well as keeping up with your learning in the classroom, college will be come easier and more enjoyable.

I had to learn this as I approached my first day of Econometrics. It had been 20 years since I had placed out of Calculus. She asked each person what was their level of Calculus knowledge compared to the rest of the class. I said it was a 2 out of 10 because I did not know my classmates and their backgrounds. I knew the basic principles but I was out of practice. I knew this going into the class because of the research I did. I wanted to become a champion and hoist the trophy. I did finish that class and await the final grade. Over half of the classed dropped out, they did not even make the playoffs. I got to play in the championship and will go for back to back titles in time series . Perception is reality, if you back it up with work ethic and a mind to explore the unknown.

"Everything I do is for my people."

 - Sacagawea

Date: May 1788 - December 20, 1812

Location: North Dakota to the Pacific Ocean

    I learned that I love people in meeting other in college. I am a people person and I love to meet and greet everyone. But you do have a close circle of people? It is human nature and I learned that your best friends accept you for who you are, tell you your flaws, and just enjoy your company without money. Sometimes this close-knit group is family, but not always. I learned Christ's blood is thicker than water. My family in Christ looks out for me; my immediate family does not.

    Sacagawea loved the Shoshone tribe and her travels further her knowledge of her tribe as well as great diplomatic relations with other indigenous peoples to the Americas as well as new settlers. There was an ugly side to this as she was captured and forced into marriage. Her children were only treated with a little respect because they had white blood flowing through them.

    She was so influential as she helped the United States decide that the Louisiana Purchase was a great investment. Realize she died when she was 24 years young. She was an interpreter of many languages, a master horticulturist, and a peace keeper between the indigenous populations that saved the lives of the white settlers that would take over; even her own tribe lands. She was only worried about her circle of people, and she got taken advantage of by racism. Don't let your Crew judge the same way. Your life will be wasted like hers was by invading entities.

"Salí mi cabeza en Madrid, Salí mi corazón en Barcelona, y Salí mi estomago in Sevilla"

- Forest D Bynum

Date: June 20, 2015

Location: riding the bus home from work

I love going to my culinary homeland. Louisiana is home for me but Spain is an experience that has taken a lifetime to appreciate. I still learn more each day but of all the countries I have traveled to, Spain is the one I learned the most, had the most fun, and yearn to continue to discover.

Madrid is like any other capital city for the first ten minutes or so with its labyrinth of subways and thousands upon millions of residents scurrying across the avenidas to live this strange thing call life. I discovered great museums and delicious food but it has become an international city and has absorbed a world culture feeling while retaining its Old World charm.

Barcelona is a place of culture within culture. It also has a great art scene and the international feel like Madrid, but a difference of a generational linguistic past summoned from commerce of the seas and the pride of a medieval kingdom. It is the hub of Spaniard business but also of the largest open market in Europe and a language that is complicated but defines a region and a people unique to Spain.

Seville was so laid back as the hot summer sun is quenched by the simple dishes of salmorejo and a plate of manzanilla olives and fresh baked bread. It tells the tale of a rich culture of Arabian influence but is just as much as a part of Spain as its brothers up north. I particularly enjoyed walks in the park of Plaza de España that transported me to a galaxy far, far away.

My first night in Spain I ran around over the double shot of espresso I purchased. I got back to my hotel at 4am and left again at 8am for breakfast. I fell in love with the Catalan culture as I saw masterpieces in a free park and at the city beach I frolicked with beautiful maidens in the moonlight. Every bite from the Valencia orange to the saffron of Consegura is perfumed in the cuisine in the south and I filled my tummy to the max. When you are in college, you need to take advantage of every opportunity. If you are blessed to go to Study Abroad, do it. You will learn a little about love , life, and the pursuit of deliciousness. Plus you can earn credit towards your degree, pleased go to class more than you go out for tapas.

"No matter what people tell you, words and ideas can change the world."

- Robin Williams

Date: July 21, 1951 - August 11, 2014
Location: Unknown

It amazes me that a man who predominate function in society was to make people laugh. He has a colorful array of movies, TV shows, and plays that depict this attitude of pleasing the crowd. He also did some serious roles as well making him a complete thespian. His thoughts to me did have a serious tone to life as you should laugh a lot in life. You know laughter is an easy way to lose weight!

This is a serious statement. What you say can have real influence on your peers, the university, and the world as a whole. Be mindful of your speech as you do your daily diligence in your scholastic achievements. Words can hurt people and they may have the wrong view of who you are. But when you use words of wisdom and careful selection, you can change the world in a positive way.

You do not have to be a wordsmith like Steven A. Smith but working on your vocabulary may be an investment worth considering. I enjoy learning new words especially in Spanish. I like to write the new words down and look them up later when I review my notes. Yes, you should not only be in class to take notes, but also review them as you go along. Sometimes when you take notes, you will realize it may not be on the test but it could enrich your word bank of life.

"El apetito de los argentinos por la cultura y la educación está, pero hay que saciarlo"

– Luísa Valenzuela

Date: November 26, 1938 - Present

Location: Somewhere in Argentina

This quote from the author of Tango, a short story I read in my language and culture class speaks about a prostitute that tells the tale of two lives, one that has accomplished her goal and the one struggling to make it any way possible. The story summarizes how the lower classes learned about getting ahead and enjoying the better way of life through sacrifice of themselves. The prostitute Sonia winds up being washed up and used in order to gain the riches of the upper class but at the cost of Sondra's soul. The author is telling us by this quote is that most Argentineans do not have access to this due to lack of funding. They do not make the willing sacrifices to get ahead by relying on government sources to give them access to art and education, usually only enjoyed by the higher class of society.

As growing up in a lower socio-economic status, I understood this when I first went to college, but realized that I needed resources. But when I traveled to Argentina in 2006, I saw the reality that I was better off than most citizens of Earth. Learning is not so expensive but formal learning where companies recognize your achievement costs a lot. I made a lot of money during my time in healthcare administration. I got to learn a lot about art and education, but I realized that I should have been making a lot more because every job I held since 2005 was a college degree level job. I was bamboozled by the fact I could self teach myself so much. When I went back to school in 2017, so many people were against me going back until they realized I did very well and I just validated what I already knew.

"It is only those who have neither fired a shot nor heard the shrieks and groans of the wounded who cry aloud for blood, more vengeance, more desolation. War is hell."

- Col. William Tecumseh Sherman

Date:

Location:

I do not what war is about, but I know it allows me to have the freedom to go back to college for redemption. He fought for his beliefs which some would say are controversial, but he helped found Louisiana State University. It's not just a university, it's my university! So, I am grateful of his contributions to education even though he wanted to continue slavery because he believed in states' rights and smaller governments.

This message he tells us is the ones who did not fight the battles were the ones deciding if war was necessary or not. Most of the men who fought in the Civil War did not have full rights as citizens. This was a scuffle that was started in the staterooms and banquet halls. It is obvious that slaves did not have voting rights, but as students, we are not slaves for we choose to grind it out in the books and the libraries to learn and discover new ground.

College is about choices in some ways. You will

have to understand there are certain regulations that you can't really have a say or debate. You just have to fight those battles as you come. I personally do not like finals to be worth more than 25% of your final grade. It just puts too much stress on finals week. I rather would demonstrate my knowledge through the semester. The problems of a few will not be attended so as to appease the whole. Shaquille O'Neal got fouled so many times in his NBA career where he would not get calls. The officials did not call them because the game would literally stop at every possession if they did, so he learn how to power through it and learn how to make the shot with the fouls. During his MVP years, he only made shots within 2 feet of the basket to have one of the higher field goal percentages in NBA history. Sometimes you just have to power through situation you do not like.

"Just one look at you and I know it's gonna be a lovely day"

– Bill Withers

Date: December 16, 1977

Location: The album "Menagerie" was published in 1978

I love the ladies, but for who they are as much as they look like. I do admire physical beauty, but it last about five minutes. Booty is in the eye of the beholder, but true beauty lasts eternally. That look is into her soul as much as it is on her lovely curves. As men, be appreciative of what a woman stands for. And for the ladies, show a man you are more than just something to look at, because you are not just a showpiece.

Keep focus on your books and don't make quick for one-night stands and frivolous dating. Find someone special and invest in them to find value in that person just like a good businessperson always does. Too many times young people jump into something and do not weigh the consequences. Are you having safe sex? Can this person teach your child to read? Do you have similar religious beliefs? Before you are fixated on their rump shaker and go spend financial aid money you don't have on expensive clothes and expensive libations, remember, you are in college and you are suppose to be just starting out.

To ensure a lovely day with a fellow companion and a potential mate, I like to use a system to prevent unwanted exposure and hurt feelings. The first time you should meet in a public place that is open with lots of people like a festival, coffee shop, or at a public library. The second time you should allow yourself a little privacy but not in your own home. The third time you meet you should be able to make a conscience decision if you want to be long term or as they use to say in the twentieth century, "steady", therefore committing yourself to one individual at a time for the pursuit of companionship and many lovely days.

"Él que lee mucho y anda mucho, ve mucho y sabe mucho."

– Miguel de Cervantes

Date: September 29, 1547 - April 22, 1616

Location: 16th century Spain

This quote from the greatest author in Hispanoamerica reminds you of the power of reading and knowledge. As students, you need to keep sharp in your craft of learning. Reading is fundamental as I learned from my childhood romps with Reggie Miller, but it can also help you advance in the business world. But reading is only part of it, you must apply what you learn to truly understand the lesson. Studying is not some chore that a wise sage developed centuries ago to take away your free time. It is to reinforce your reading and exercises given in class.

Only by reading and studying can you truly see the message come to life and know the material to mastery. Reading without studying is quixotic by nature. In my personal recollection, it is a daunting task when you have only read over the material but you have not taken the time to break it down into digestible chunks which can be disseminated into a passing score on an examination. I think I could have done better in a few classes if I took extra time to really break down the lessons.

To see and to know the material can also be true as I continue to stress the importance of class attendance. There are some academic topics I can recognize such as a partial derivative. I see it and I understand it, but I am not so accurate in solving one. On the other hand, I can actually write a balance sheet from the information I learned in my accounting classes. Even though, my major does not stress Accounting, I paid attention and I got an A in both of those courses by reading and learning.

"Reinvention is sometimes the mother of necessity"

– Forest Bynum

Date: Dec 2018

Location: at my apartment

When I eat dinner, usually it is another iteration of the original dish. I have learned to eat simply and allow base ingredients control my diet. I once did a Spanish project where I did a cooking show called Cocina con Bosque. I spent about 25 dollars of my Food Stamps on ingredients (by the way, I got a solid A-) but I did not waste a single drop. I used the leftover vegetables for stir fry and cooking holiday lentils, one of my favorite dishes that brings Old World Spain to my heritage of downhome Louisiana cuisine.

Sometimes we have to understand that knowledge is built from previous knowledge, but in some cases you can use the same knowledge in different subjects. This is what makes learning the required courses unique. These teachings are simple but can be used in many ways, to reinvent learning but using the same information you learned before. It is not wise to take on a learning style where you just memorize and forget. You never know when you need that tool from your tool kit of knowledge.

By learning how to cook before I came back to college. I was able to apply the same, simple cooking technique into a showcase of language mastery of cooking terms. I wrote the recipe from scratch in Spanish. I had to commentate the whole video in Spanish in front of my classmates. But it was just another form of pizza I already knew how to cook. Reinvention is a tool you can use sometimes to recycle basic skills, but sometimes you just have to hunker down and be attentive to the learning process.

"Poor is the pupil who does not surpass his master."

- Leonardo da Vinci

Date: April 15, 1452 - May 2, 1519

Location: Unknown

 "How did you know that was the blue one?" This is a quote from one of my favorite movies, The Last Dragon. Bruce Leroy is searching for the final level and the story starts with his master telling him that he can no longer teach him and that he must go on his next journey alone. The end of the movie comes to a self realization that he already possessed the techniques and the style to sur-pass his master. The movie reminds me of my past of finding a job to seeking new ground in cooking.

 I have spoken of my two culinary masters in this book and they are very special to me as James Wether-ford allowed me to learn the basics of French cooking in a diner setting and pick up on business techniques that I still use today. Todd Barrios exposed me to International Cuisine and several techniques including basic butchery, fish preparation, and preparing for large numbers of guests. I took that knowledge and was able to travel Latin America and fell in love with the cuisine of Spain. My style of cooking has developed into Iberian-Latin cuisine where the techniques of Old World Spain are influenced by the flavors of Mexico, Caribbean, plus Central and South America.

So when you are sitting in class and saying to yourself, "This is so boring, why am I here?" Remind yourself that you need to learn enough to where you can make contributions to higher learning and in the corporate world and surpass your teachers. You can start the process with the mindset of getting "A's" instead of passing. When you get an A in a class, it lets everyone know you have mastery of the subject. You will touch the final level and get to... the degree.

"Para un pueblo hambriento e inactivo, la única forma en la que Dios puede aparecer es en la de comida y trabajo."

- Miguel Ángel Asturias

Date: October 19, 1899 - June 9, 1974

Location: Unknown

      I know a lot about being poor, hungry, and no work and a big shout out to the true starving artists. Asturias was a true artist winning the Nobel Peace Prize in 1967 for his work Men of Maize. He was of a well to do family that observed many traditions of the indigenous peoples and was celebrated for writing about such topics around the world. Through these writings, he expressed a sentiment of the struggles of the native peoples to find work and supporting themselves. I also have experienced the troubles of finding work and being able to eat. I have been homeless and understand a small part of the discrimination and disadvantages of someone who is unwanted in society.

      I want to let you know that there are struggles in college including the delicate balance of nutrition, sustenance, and income. College kids need to eat, but scholars can't live off pizza alone. We all know that pizza is filling and cheap, if you buy it frozen. The balance comes in where you want to buy a delivery pizza knowing it will exhaust the coffers of your part time work study position. Or deciding maybe you should eat rice and vegetables instead of pizza everyday. I know it is tough, but having a little work in college allows for the splurge every once in a while.

I am so blessed as I went through some rough times medically and I relied on the great folks at a food giveaway through my campus. I would not have finished the semester without it. Because of my medical emergency, I was not able to work and found that meat sometime became a luxury when the Food Stamp office decided that I was not going to receive Food Stamps anymore. The indigenous folks in his tales did not have any opportunities to find work to be able to eat good food let alone higher education. A little work will help out your nutrition a long way. And...eat your vegetables already!

"When I get a little money I buy books; and if any is left I buy food and clothes."

- Desiderius Erasmus

Date: October 28, 1466 - July 12, 1536

Location: Unknown

A man that embraced the idea of Protestantism but held on to the traditions of the Catholic Church was known for being a scholar for most of his life. He understood the importance of books as he lived during the Reformation where the printing press allowed for the mass distribution of knowledge.

He understood the importance of education during his stays in England, Paris, and Basel. He was a bit of a traveling man like myself and understood the necessities of life. He was devoted to learning and put books as priority and sustenance as secondary. Like any college student, he liked a drink of wine and was known to have a special corkscrew for his chosen drink of sousery. He accomplished many things and helped the Catholic Church into the 16th century.

Budgeting beyond books is key to be able to get the degree we so desire. Spending money on books is mandatory as I am told of this method of buying both the digital and print books. I would think it would be exactly the same but some texts do include portions in the digital. I would like the convenience of having both if I could afford it as if your computer is down or if it is dependent on the Internet, you would have a backup. Also I am starting to realize I should keep some of these textbooks for reference. I think I may go back and buy a few for the future. Buying books is important, but remember to read them to get that degree.

"You know, you do need mentors, but in the end, you really just need to believe in yourself."

– Diana Ross

Date: March 26, 1944 - Present

Location: Unknown

When I decided to come back to school. I realized very quickly that I needed help to navigate the 21st century land of academia. The idea of all my textbooks being digital and the necessity of a current smartphone came to a blazing reality as I was lost without the direction of the Google Maps of higher education. I tried to find specifically a mentor and I found several, my professors. I realized that asking for help and being attentive goes a long way as they will guide you in learning and in the ways of life. I always make sure to shake their hand and thank them at the end of each semester for their contribution to my development.

I also have been able to find certain people that do encourage and help me solve some of the indirect academic issues that occur. Sometimes a procedure or a process is not clear or you just need to find the right source of information. As being an older student, it does feel weird but I have to rely upon a lot of younger individuals to navigate the waterways and ride the waves of the college process to reach the sunny tropical island of graduation.

At the end of the day, a mentor will help navigate but you must do the work of pulling the rope to move the sails to guide the ship. You must learn how to operate the astrolabe of discovery so that you can be a captain one day to help others and be the conquistador of your field. If you want to ride in the sunset in a galleon instead of a row boat, utilize others help, but rely on the sweat of your own brow.

"I like to cook with the philosophy of using great ingredients and not altering them too much."

- Aaron Sanchez

Date: February 12, 1976 - Present

Location: Unknown

This is a simple but complex concept I learned over time. It started by having a great cook in my father who made great New Orleans Italian cuisine and my mother whose food was rather lackluster. The difference was fresh ingredients. When I was in my twentysomethings, I learned how to cook well, and it better suited my health, my budget, and my overall wellbeing. Learning how to cook simple food is a task but one worth taking. Eating out every day is not good, and you will be a better college student if you heed his advice. You do not have to use a complicated recipe in order to eat, just learn simple techniques like the art of the stir fry and how to roast a chicken.

I have learned that cooking is done by artists by baking is done by scientists. When you bake something, always follow the recipe and be aware of certain modifications like substitutions and elevation that can ruin a good plate of food. Having good shopping habits also help by purchasing ingredients with value. It may be worth it to visit that produce stand or the particular bakery to get goodness out of you dietary purchase. When I lived near a produce stand, it allowed me to be able to fill more of my diet with local produce which is cheaper, riper, and just plain delicious. My overall health improved as well. Now whenever I am looking for something to eat, I strive for purchases with simple food that have monetary value that are easy to eat. I also have to look for the nutritional value I crave and my body needs. I like sushi, but I rather purchase the banana and the cheese sandwich for every-day consumption.

" Remember, there is more to life then where you came from, there is always adventure."

Forest Bynum

Date: approximately Jan 1st, 2011

Location: Unknown

I came from a poor background. There was not dinner everyday on the table. My mother would shop in bargain bins for school clothes. The public library was our babysitter. It took me almost 30 years to realize what I had done. I could actually look back and seen what I had accomplished. I was in the process of researching recipes. I was plaza hoppin' across the globe. I had great friends and good times. But I still was looking for more adventure. Realize before I left home at 17, I barely left the State of Louisiana. At this point I had visited 20 countries on 4 continents. I was blessed to be able to experience there is more to this life than to be stuck at the level of my upbringing.

As college students, you will come from a particular socio-economic status. Whether you are rich or poor, I challenge you to sit down and think of one place you would want to go and see for yourself. It could be just a few miles or in another hemisphere. Take one hour to plan it out and try to come up with a timeline and a rudimentary budget. Next, find one person who believes in you and will not discourage you as I want every college student before they graduate to go on at least one adventure of a lifetime.

This is not the same as a family vacation or a spring break romp where a bottle of vodka is attached to the shower head (I never actually done this but heard of such scary tales)… do not do that by the way, just be civilized and take shots with grapefruit soda with a great friend you met from a land down under. I did actually do that and after we finished the first, I was exhausted but I was glad to spend Christmas in a land where the indigenous speak a beautiful language I personally got to learn one word in Mayan.

I challenge your adventure have an educational aspect in it. You may never know when you need to write a paper on an experience or you meet a hot chica and have something to talk about. Trust on this where there is more than you came from, because I am living proof that even a pariah can become a world traveler.

"A bold bet doesn't assure you of winning, but if you make no bold bets you can't continue to succeed."

- Steve Ballmer

Date: 2012

Location: Microsoft's Worldwide Partner Conference

I have many mistakes in my life, so have most people. You have to learn by your mistakes, but you can't play life conservative all the time, at some point, you make gambles. I made the biggest gamble of my life by going back to school with no job, no money, and no place to live. I lived in the crummiest week by week in you could imagine filled with characters of ill repute and suspect actions of violence and illegal drugs. I charged it on a credit card but was successful as I made straight A's that semester to get accepted to LSU.

My gamble is still not over. I still am awaiting acceptance into the College of Business. Because of my past mistakes, my overall business GPA at LSU is a 2.52, but my business core is a 3.5. In other words, I have to continue to produce at a Dean's List level just to keep my spot at the university. But I am glad that I slept on the streets. That I caught the bus at 5:45 AM to get to my 7:30 Spanish class on time. That I saved my money during the Fall of 2017 to go to the Dominican Republic. All of these were calculated gambles that were needed for me to progress as a college student.

As you complete your classes and figure out what life is about, you will need to make some gambles. Solidify your major and take the challenging classes. Look for opportunities for undergrad research. Find avenues to learn during the semester breaks including internships and summer jobs. You may need to take a few calculated gambles to let the odds of life to be forever in your favor. When you have that degree in your hand and your friend sprays you with silly string and says, "I will need the same treatment next year when I graduate!"

"Size doesn't make any difference; heart is what makes a difference."

– Jerry Sloan

Date: March 28, 1942 - Present

Location: Vivint Smart Home Arena

I have to remind myself all the time that caring about what I do is just as important as how much I do. If you want to accomplish goals, like making Dean's List or becoming a leader on campus, you must learn to overcome adversities like the size of someone else's checkbook or physique. Jerry Sloan was one of the best NBA coaches of all time and lead the Utah Jazz to back to back Finals appearances. Sometimes making an A or a C in a class is finding out how to make the playoffs, putting yourself in position to win the championship. I try to take away something from every class I take, even the required ones so that I can claim victory for Christ for helping me put in the hard work. I needed to take a biology class, and I was not looking forward to it, but I found interesting topics within the lessons to make my heart be in the class.

When you come to college, you will realize there is someone there that is smarter, stronger, or has more resources than you, but that does not mean you can't be successful. Sometimes, it is not as big as an advantage as you think. It can change the personality of a student for the worst to rely on just previous knowledge or techniques. Get out of the high school way of thinking. College is the great equalizer, and when you push yourself for the degree, you will have acquired greatness no matter the GPA. Because you will have to apply yourself to make that degree worth value and play in the game of the playoffs of life, disposable income. If you keep your priorities in check, finding employment with your degree will be rewarding and you may just hoist a trophy or two.

"The purpose of art is washing the dust of daily life off our souls."

- Pablo Picasso

Date: October 25, 1881 - April 8, 1973

Location: Unknown

One of the most memorable moments in traveling to Spain is when I got to visit the Reina Sofia. I made a stop in Madrid before coming come from Seville in 2015 to go to this museum that houses some of Picasso's work. I saw history come to life as I witness Guernica, a paint that reflects the artist view of the Civil War in Spain. I got to see a piece of history with its muted grays and blacks with the occasional speck of color as the masterpiece came to life. It is a testament to how traveling is good for the soul. That day, art cleansed me of daily life and gave me insight into the rich culture of Spain.

My eyes opened when I went to the Museum of Modern Art in San Jose, Costa Rica. I got to see a copper etching that was from the floor to the arched ceilings about the Old Testament stories. There also was a weird exhibit about taking black and white photos and covering them with colored screens. It was so fascinating and it cost me 50 cents. From then on, I made it a point to check out Modern Art as well as the well known painters to dust myself off of the perception that new art is not great art.

As college students, you will realize that art is everywhere and even though Pablo may have been different, his techniques are time honored and well documented. You will come across it in every aspect of learning because it stimulates the human mind and shapes society because to the different interpretations that come out of experiencing the visually appealing. Take time to look at through all types of media, because your teachers will use it to get your attention.

"It is better to excel in any single art than to arrive only at mediocrity in several."

– Pliny the Younger

Date: 61 AD - 113 AD

Location: height of the Roman Empire (Pax Romana)

Focus in college is a key factor in success. A general studies degree shows that you can pay attention to the teacher. A real degree can prepare you for a job or an exciting career. I have lots of abilities and skills. I would never become an artist, but I can design something in Photoshop or even draw a sketch with a pencil, but a true artist masters his craft.

In the Roman times, you specialized in something as part of the upper class. He was a lawyer, so his strength was law, but he did other things as well. I tell you if you are going to go to college, have a focus and talk to your advisors about your specific classes. Make sure it aligns to your focus and it does not become busy work. Challenge yourself even with your electives and get the most out of your degree and your tuition payment.

Mediocrity will only allow you to escape the pain of worthless classes and no degree. College is a time of specialization. For those who know what they want, companies hire them because they are better prepared for the marketplace. For a few that are really smart and don't have a direction, a company may help them, but most companies are looking for polished products in their human capital. Be ready to defend your transcript for that management position out of college.

"Expectation is the mother of all frustration."

-- Antonio Banderas

Date: August 10, 1960 - Present

Location: Unknown

I know people expect me to do well in school. I let them down. My high school teachers. My father. My former boss. I believed the hype when I was homeless and was trying to find work. There were a few organizations that said I would never make it back to finish school. It was very frustrating indeed. People make assumptions about you but that is not how you have to live your life. Your closest circle will want you to perform in college, but what is most important is that you do your best.

So now that you are in college, people will still have these expectations. You have to be careful of being pushed around too much. You do not have to let your parents live their life vicariously through you, but also remember to be mindful of your purpose especially if they help you pay your tuition. Lots of students want to carry on a legacy performed by their parents but are not cut out for the same profession. I even have expectations for you. You are the next generation and while I age into retirement, you will be at your employment peak. I want you to do your best, but what you want to do it to contribute to society. So if you want to become a movie star, that is great, but be ready for rejection. I am sure Mr. Banderas experienced his fair share as he left his hometown of Malaga for his shot at the silver screen. Malaga is a nice place to visit, but I like only the expectation of 330 days of sunny skies, I rather live at home in Louisiana.

" How ruthless a thug is to prey on the humble avocado farmer and steal the precious warmth and hospitality of a nation? "

- Forest Bynum

Date: During the 21st century

Location: travels in Mexico

I love traveling to Mexico, especially by bus. It is a different world when you get south of Mexico D.F. To get there, you have to travel through cartel infused states that want to make money and not invest in the great citizens of Mexico. When I first started to go to Mexico, you could buy avocadoes ten for a dollar, and sometimes for free as they would lay on the ground in someone's yard. As Mexican food became popular in the beginning of the 21st century, the price of avocadoes increased in the United States. It was such a profitable good, gangs took over farms by force.

Travel is really tough now by bus, and it is so dangerous, I no longer can make the journeys by bus. The Mexican government is finally making strides to push these thugs out to give back these people their land back and to stabilize a crop that grows the Mexican GDP. Avocadoes are a part of my diet with its richness in omega-3 fatty acids and its wonderful creamy taste.

Learning about current events is a great tool for

college students. It grooms you to be responsible citizens and help you form opinions. You can sift the truth out of sensationalism and you can formulate your won world view based on fact and knowledge. It hurts my soul that a thug would actually switch from selling drugs to avocadoes until you realize that it not only promotes the distribution of illegal drugs but takes jobs from worthy people and a fun pastime for myself. I still have a few cities I want to see in Mexico, but until it is safe enough, I can only visit by plane.

"There are no borders between ingredients"

- Rokusaburo Michiba

Date: January 3, 1931 - Present

Location: Japan

This is one of the many people who I look up to from my favorite TV show Iron Chef. In 1993 he faced talented chefs in an arena with unlimited bounds as he took a French ingredient foie gras and made it Japanese. His talents expressed in his dishes challenges the superstition of using certain ingredients of one style of cooking. He is truly an academic and someone that inspired me to extended my eating habits beyond the ordinary.

Experimenting with recipes and food is fun and I recommend maybe trying something with a different approach. College has this type of approach, it really has no borders. Learning should bring you to discover your own creations in a stadium of learning. There is a time clock as these superior chefs face to put for the new dishes of history by realizing the best meal is completed by obtaining a degree.

So do you dare to venture outside the boundaries of your discipline? These brave chefs put their reputation on the line as they discover new ground while wearing a silly costume and be involved in a pageantry and rivalry that makes the Japanese version the best because they took no expense to perfect their craft. Many other countries took their model but it is not quite the same as they embedded the culture into the show. Bring your knowledge and passion outside the realm of your classroom projects and into the corporate boardroom. Using knowledge in all aspects of your life will make it easier to get your degree. Will your cuisine reign supreme?

"I have gathered a posie of other men's flowers, and nothing but the thread that binds them is mine own"

- John Bartlett

Date: June 14, 1820 - December 3, 1905

Location: Unknown

This is a very special person that inspires me to read and write. His quote explains how his life was searching for wisdom. He has written the largest collection of quotations in American history. We can take the lesson of Mr. Bartlett and apply it to the social media of the day as he uses vernacular of the common time to express his life's achievements.

Sometime social media is positive, but it can also be negative. Remember to use social media for its intended use. Keeping in touch with your friends is a great ways to use Facebook. Keeping in touch with the Kardashians may not be the best investment of your time in college. Monitoring snowflakes on The Weather Channel app with Watson is exciting especially when Baton Rouge comes on the radar. Monitoring snowflakes disappear as you swipe to the right on dating sites may not be so beneficial to your study habits. Mr. Bartlett obviously enjoyed collecting wise tidbits, but you should also heed warning to people who mouth off nonsense.

You still have to use common sense. I carefully selected quotes to learn positive morals and not to negatively influence the masses. Be careful with social media and do not let it obsess your life. Even some of the messages that Bartlett published were out of the ordinary. The impact was so beneficial, he has become an icon in philosophical circles.

"My future starts when I wake up every morning. Every day I find something creative to do with my life."

- Miles Davis

Date: May 26, 1926 - September 28, 1991

Location: Unknown

I am an early riser and I love to seize the day. My experience from attending college is that some things are mundane like following the same schedule. You should go to everyone of your classes each week but have something else to look forward to each day. Life lessons are learned usually when the unexpected occurs in your life. I had to learn this the hard way, but you should try to schedule fun periodically through the week but keep up with your work.

No matter how hard you work in school and learn your studies, creativity is something special and should be cherished as you live life each day. Some of the most rewarding days of life have come through being creative. I am a student but I also like to write and create recipes. A doodling with colored pencils or crayon is fun every once in a while especially if it is on your economics homework. In this life, you can't plan for everything, but you should have the attitude of wanting to live life each day and find the creative spark in the moment.

Creative moments are easy for those who major in art and music, but what about the rest of us. You can be creative in your business degree, pre med studies, or even imitating a hook shot from your favorite basketball start. Life is too short to live a sedentary life. Be creative, it just may get you a job one day.

"The greatest glory in living lies not in never falling, but in rising every time we fall."

- Ralph Waldo Emerson

Date: May 25, 1803 - April 27, 1882

Location: Unknown

Well, I have encountered so many setbacks in life, but having the ability to try again is not always present in the classroom. Strike early and on the first test or assignment, try to aim high to set the tone instead of trying to recover a passing grade at the end of the semester. It is OK if you make mistakes or don't understand. But to rise up in the collegiate levels, you will have to humble yourself and find a tutor or a different plan of attack for studying or completing classwork.

In college, there is no such thing as the dog ate your homework. You have to develop responsibility, but at the same time remember to fight back when you make a bad grade in a class. I receive a 38 F on one of my first collegiate test in microeconomics. It took a special lady who let me sleepover and study 3 days straight to pass that class with a C by aceing the final.

There is something to say about someone who never gives up. In the workplace, there are mistakes to be made and you will fail. In your studies you will have setbacks as well. Take these issues and learn from them to accomplish the overall agenda of your stay at college, to get the degree. Believe it or not, most students fail at least one course before they finish, but perseverance will prevail once you realize that the end result is what employer will count for your evaluation.

"And how much better to die in all the happy period of undisillusioned youth, to go out in a blaze of light, than to have your body worn out and old and illusions shattered."

- Ernest Hemingway

Date: October 18, 1918

Location: Milan, Italy

     I always kid around with my friends that if I am not going to succeed in something that I am going to go out in a blaze of glory. I speak of my faith in Christ Jesus in that if something doesn't work out, I am always going to keep the faith and never renounce it for anything in the world. Even though I may be worn down and down trodden, it will not shake my faith. Realizes the times I have been homeless, without a home, I always had Christ.

     Hemingway who used his travels to influence his writing style composed himself in a way that while he was young, he would live life to the fullest. Based on his wide spectrum of work, I would suspect he always considered himself living young even while he was the Old Man at the Sea. By exploring the world, life was never an illusion because he was knew what was going on in the world around him and my travels have treated me the same.

     For us college students we must appreciate the

worldview as we are shown the theory in most of our classes but are expected to perform in the practical as we collect our scrolls from the stage. One must remember to take advantage of the college years and expand their worldview and not just live in a bubble of theory, because life does not work that way. Life is not lived in a vacuum, there is always a friction coefficient. Do not be disillusioned by the perfect job, the perfect spouse, the perfect home. You may find yourself out of reality if you don't live life for your best efforts but realize the world is not perfect. I am 38 years young, and I still have to remind myself of this daily.

"Viva pobre, sea rico"

- Forest Bynum

Date: November 22, 2018

Location: Allen Parish Behavioral Unit

I like the simple things in life. A stroll down the street to the green grocer. A conversation with the lady at the post office. A glass of lemonade with the kid that cuts your grass. These are beautiful and when you do not have a lot of money. Simple things are cherished.

Now imagine being strapped down in a stretcher when your known diagnosis was hypertension. Your belongings confiscated. You are taken to a place you did not know existed. They take you into a place where they pass out cigarettes to patients. The food is barely edible. You have to wear socks for ten days where the heater does not work. I came across this message when I realized how blessed life really was on the outside. This quote uses the subjunctive tense that most American do not recognize in their speech. You should live poor in order to be rich. To be rich in culture, character, and charisma.

As a college student, most of are poor, but a few

are blessed to have money. Money is a necessary unit of measure in society, but it is not the only thing. You should pursue to earn a great living to make a secure life for yourself. You should also remember that throwing money at something doesn't always make it better. I have learned that some of the poorest of people live full lives through my travels. I know today from these experiences that I am rich. So remember, live poor but be rich in good attitude, effort at school, and treating others. The psych ward was not so bad. I did make it out alive, read some good books, wrote an econometric model, and got to color with crayons as I thought how I was going to battle high blood pressure and pass the semester.

"To know that we know what we know, and to know that we do not know what we do not know, that is true knowledge."

- Nicolaus Copernicus

Date: February 19, 1473 - May 24, 1543

Location: Unknown

This may seem to be a tongue twister, but it is pretty much straight forward. Being able to tell the difference between right and wrong starts when we are young but is highly recommended at college. But what right is right? What wrongs are really wrong? The degree of morality is an issue you will face but you always have to be true to yourself in judgement calls. I mean, who has time to measure the handbook that a university publishes each year but no student has time to read. It is not to say the precedents set forth by a learning institution is bad, but that common sense plays a huge part in this debate in the scales of balancing the duality of the correct action to choose.

His mathematical concepts were right but are still theory because no one owns a rope long enough to measure the solar system or durable enough to get close enough to the Sun to take a picture to put on Instagram. Just think before his time, people thought the world was flat and the moon was the best guide to measure time on a calendar.

Heed the warnings of everything you here has to be correct. College allows us to challenge the status quo but also be respectful when you realize you bet on the wrong side, no matter who is the moderator in your life. You can't be lukewarm in opinion and become a double agent. This is how you play the game in college, the academic game. One of the aspects is to choose a side, develop a case, and prove that it is correct, making mere theory a fact of life. I did not have to fact check that with Mrs. Garrett.

"Divide each difficulty into as many parts as is feasible and necessary to resolve it."

- Rene Descartes

Date: March 31, 1596 - February 11, 1650

Location: Unknown

I remember from learning Calculus of the graph of shapes and from this method of analytic geometry we could explore the possibilities of integrals. Starting with simple shapes we could derive ordinary geometric objects such as the cone, pyramid, and the sphere. From this you can use deductive reasoning to take the graph of a circle rotating around an imaginary axis to create the Homer Simpson special treat not made from the wonderful, magical animal. The torus is something you have to use several steps to calculate the volume, but once understood, can sweeten the realm of complex mathematics.

Your brain thinks like this intuitively. Rules for the direction of mind can only happen step by step like a computer program. For easy tasks, you just complete them very quickly. But how about the research paper? The group presentation? Memorizing the bones of the body? This takes several steps and requires planning and careful thought. College presents us lots of new challenges that you can't do the night before and expect to do well.

You may pass but passing allows you only to be at the bottom of the professional ranks. High achievers make decisions like planning through the semester to tackle large projects that include writing steps and dates to complete each part. If any of your classes involved the scientific method, this thought of dividing tasks is crucial to find a solution to your hypothesis. This is not to waste time in the observation and the collection of data. Take you time and break tasks to its simplest form to ensure success.

"A child who is allowed to be disrespectful to his parents will not have true respect for anyone."

- Billy Graham

Date: November 7, 1918 - February 21, 2018

Location: Unknown

Your parents are very influential in the upbringing of your college career. My father passed away and my mother was not very supportive of my decision of going to college. That is out of the ordinary, but I still respected my parents and you should as well. This quote is not hiding anything and you should appreciate everything that your parents provide for your education.

Parents, you are not off the hook. Just because you are free from your child from your home, doesn't mean you give up on them. Even if you do not have money, I am sure you can find a roll of quarters for laundry. Make a batch of that favorite macaroni and cheese for your child. Write them letters of encouragement. Your kids need your strength and your advice. If you know about money, help them with their finances. If you don't, find someone who does. I am sick and tired of seeing students who have parents that don't contribute. Just because they are 18, doesn't mean you stop loving them.

Fellow students, as an elder statesmen, I plead to you that you should keep in touch with your folks. You do not have to go home every weekend, but visit them and thank them for everything. When you graduate, I strongly suggest you buy a thank you card and actually write your own heart felt message. If you do not heed my advice, you may find yourself without a mate, people do marry their family as well. Don't leave a trail of disrespect because you think you are grown, but be humble, for some students don't have parents to help them at all.

"Keep doing some kind of work, that the devil may always find you employed"

- Saint Jerome

Date: March 27, 347 AD - September 30, 420 AD

Location: Unknown

One of the mistakes I made when I first started college in 1998 was that I did not have a job. I think a part time job would have helped me stay focused, be part of the university, and given me some needed resources to complete my degree when I was young. Now that I am older, I enjoy the sweat of my brow and the feeling of a good hard day's work for my duly wages.

Men, let's go deeper into this subject, because you should want to have that urge to support a household one day. You also probably deal with the enticement of beautiful eligible ladies that take court in your classrooms, libraries, and quadrangles. It is fun to meet women, flirt about the frolicking students to get yourself in the lottery for the eventful box socials of the day, and perhaps get to know a special someone in a long lasting relationship. But some boys choose the alternative of normal social progression and treat women as pin ups, divulge in the digital dating and voyeurism, and commit personal acts of self satisfaction that hinder future reproduction and put the female body as an impossible goal unattainable even by the best plastic surgeon that can augment or specialize in numerous ways of plasty. By creating this fantastical, whimsical, Barbie doll playland; they lose touch of what a real woman is and miss out on work experience and monetary gain albeit a small gain.

By finding a part time job, it will help keep you out of trouble, help with social status, and can be used to progress your career after you obtain your degree. Trust me, it is very hard to meet a lady of reputable stature if you can't even afford to buy her a five dollar coffee. This will keep the devil from corrupting your life.

"Julio said, "I will make all the wine you can sell," and Ernest replied, "I will sell all the wine you can make."

- Ernest and Julio Gallo

Date: 1933

Location: Napa Valley, California

A business lesson for everyone to learn many basic principles to achieve success. They took advantage of a time period where Prohibition had just entered and the drought in the beginning of the twentieth century had ended. Obvious Julio was the operations manager and Ernest was the marketing manager. They took an Old World product and gave new life to wine drinking in the US and eventually became a international distributor of a variety of wines.

My dad was a fan of the Vermouth they produced. He drank about 6 times a year on a holiday. He pulled a glass out the china cabinet, put a couple of cubes of ice, and sipped a couple of glasses before bed. I learned self control of adult beverages from these precious moments. This is a very important lesson I want to share for all of those in college. Drinking is a very serious topic and you should always obey any laws in your area. Some people would say the Gallo brothers should not advertise large consumption but they are just promoting good business.

As individuals we need to take charge of our social life and charge it to ourselves to limit our alcohol consumption.

   With that warning being said, wine is absolutely delicious and I would be lying if I told the tales of prevention and I did not tell you the reality of the college world. People drink. It is a legal drug and too much is always harmful, but so is drinking everyday. It does not help in school work and you should only drink to celebrate, never when you are depressed because alcohol is a depressant. I personally like deep reds, unblended, preferably from Spain or Argentina, but a California Zinfadel is great to sip with friends every once in a while. The Gallo brothers brought value to a great American product and you are a great product as well. Treat yourself that way and be careful. Never drink alone. Never drive when consuming alcohol. Don't drink in an area where you are not familiar. Make sure no one puts something in your drink, if you walk away from it, pour it out! Drinking is college is a long tradition, but let's stop being stupid about it and be responsible. The most important advice I can give you about drinking is you should enjoy the taste of what you are drinking. By the way, coffee is still my favorite drink, but wine is a close second.

"Save the World, Pursue Love and Live, Get Money (not necessarily in that order)"

- Forest D. Bynum

Date: October 2018

Location: 5116 Highland Road Apt 77A

Life is about priorities. You can get consumed by being the super hero or the televangelist. You can become the neighborhood Casanova or the Tim Meadows on the block. You can be the next prophet of profit or make yourself a bizness, man or just a businessman. These hats you have to change periodically to maximize your potential and keep your sanity and wits contained. You are the haberdasher of your life that controls your fate and the percentage that influences your life with the shoes you fill.

I encourage everyone to volunteer and think of the greater good for a worth cause. Use what you have learned in the classroom and apply to help the less fortunate, you may be assisting a future CEO in the process. You should pursue love in a careful but meaningful way. If you can find the right mate while you are young, you can grow old and make mistakes together to be a long lasting couple. I made the mistake of stop pursuing dating for about 7 years till I came back to college. I made me realize that I could love a woman again and, more importantly, that someone could love me. Live life to the fullest, each day is very precious, raise up and get your travel on, and respect everyone along the way. I live life through daily prayer, reading of the Word, and worshipping Christ

Let's not be naïve to the fact that it takes money to do most of these functions. Sometimes we do have to put the dream factory on hold until we punchout the timeclock. Earning money is not evil if it is use for finding true love, living a good life, or helping others. Sometimes flip flopping priorities occurs on a daily basis, but you have the power to choose the order.

"If you want to be successful in a particular field of endeavor, I think perseverance is one of the key qualities"

- George Lucas

Date: May 14, 1944 - Present

Location:

Finding focus in a major is very important, but it develops like the midiclorians in a young child riding an illegal speeder in a race usually ran by non humanoids. You must be in tune with yourself and what not only what you like to do, but what you are capable of doing.

Do not be afraid if you switch majors but I would suggest doing it early if you see if the concepts do not click. Do not use the excuse "I hate math" because every profession at some point uses numbers because a job will relate to money. Math makes the theory practical in most cases. Do not use the excuse " I can't write" because there are too many resources to learn and you have to be able to communicate in order to be successful.

Every major has its difficulties and there is no avoiding a difficult class or a not so agreeable teacher. Life is about obstacles and in college you have to learn how to preserve and find a way through them or around them for success. By finding a focus, you will be more marketable in the workforce and show you can handle the difficult tasks. Plus, those of you wanting to enter graduate school, finding focus is a must as the curriculum gets to be more specific and challenging. May the Forest be with you!

"Inspiration can be found in a pile of junk. Sometimes, you can put it together with a good imagination and invent something"

- Thomas Edison

Date: February 11, 1847 - October 18, 1931

Location: Unknown

     I grew up poor and buying things new always did not happen. A light bulb went off in my head when I realized that some used things have value. Thomas Edison was not only an inventor but also was a great marketer of all sorts of ideas and products. His 84 years in the world expanded the ingenuity of the American work force and how life was lived in the 20th century. Do not let the illusion of consumerism always control your life.

     Technology is something that can work used but is not optimal. Thomas Edison was a pioneer in industrial technology. Like other scientists in England that sparked the Industrial Age, he developed the first industrial research laboratory. He also had breakthroughs in other sectors as he developed one of the first motion picture cameras. I had a computer for over 6 years before it finally would not boot up consistently. But I made the Dean's List 3 times with it. Eventually, I had to invest in new technology just like Edison's work continue to grow over time. Keeping up with technology is a principle that most companies have to follow to stay competitive as all tech-nology depreciates.

However, there are other items that used may be better. If you take care of clothing, it can last several years. Used clothes are a great way to save money and reinvent yourself. So, when you shop, make sure that if you by clothes new or used, it has the best value. Name brands do not always equate to name brand quality. I buy name brand dress shirts because of the quality and size availability that I can only find online. Slacks I buy at Walmart or from second hand store. No employer has ever questioned my slacks as long as they are clean and wrinkle free. Because someone's pile of junk can help me graduate.

"I'm feelin' mighty fine…got good music on my radio"

- Charles Brown

Date: 1961

Location: Merry Christmas Baby - Sings Christmas Songs

This song brings back great memories of my father. He would play this song before we could open our Christmas gifts. Few of said traditions existed at my house. I mean, there was the Thanksgiving gumbo, and BBQ of 4th of July, but this is typical of many southern Louisiana Homes. We did not have a lot, but I always looked forward to the song because none of my other friends ever spoke of such tradition. It was an expression of my father's soul and a way to give thanks for the blessings we had. I did not grow up in a religious house, but I realized the importance of traditions.

Listening to the song, it invokes a relaxed style on the holiday of Christmas. I am not so big into the consumerism, but now that I know Christ, the tradition is more a part of my life. The birth of my Savior I do remember and I tip a glass of the ripple to my father as I hear it on Christmas Day, but I now cherish other Christian holidays more, like Easter. I take the Latin American approach and like to celebrate Holy Week.

In college, there are lots of traditions and folklore that set it apart from other areas in your life. You will see many alumni continue these traditions to let the good times be eternal. Fun traditions make life so much easier and are ways to have something to look forward to during the semester. Learn about a tradition at your college and participate.

"You've got a smile that could light up this whole town."

- Taylor Swift

Date: 2008

Location: "You Belong to Me"; Fearless Album

Sometimes you have to understand that you can only be you. This song is about pressures of young people to fit in in order to belong in society. As being a business major, I had to learn about finding your strategic competitive advantage. Your advantage can't be something you make up or create a façade. No one can't keep that up for a lifetime.

In college, your true personality will come to the forefront. You can live your wildest dreams, but you will find out who you really belong to when you are true to yourself. Yes, I am telling you that you need to market yourself. I learned that from my marketing teacher, to me she is a holy woman, but not just for marketing. She taught me about showing my true colors more than just a Cyndi Lauper ballad but as a demonstration of my talent that I have acquired over time in my college career and beyond. She also told me to relax every once and a while, enjoy the show, experience the drama, and listen to Taylor Swift. We have no bad blood, because she is someone to look up to as a great teacher and leader in the 21st century business world.

"De lo heroico a lo ridículo no hay más que un paso."

- Simon Bolivar

Date: July 24, 1783 - December 17, 1830

Location: Unknown

I have had to learn in my life about wanting to be a hero. You can't be trained to be a super hero, you just become one. I have a passion to help people and sometimes have a tendency to want to help too much. The man that shaped 19th century Latin America gives us some great advice.

He tells us that there is a thin line from being a hero to being absolutely ridiculous. When he wanted to liberate Venezuela, it was to treat his people correctly. But his grandiose ideas influenced by European writers came to light. His expansion for all Latin America to be a single entity was doomed for it was for just liberation but power and greed. It almost seems it was a botched 19th century Game of Thrones. So, put the dreams of wearing a cape and a mask away because there are several ways to achieve herodom without liberating a persecuted people.

I encourage you to volunteer. Volunteering you can become a hero or heroine of sorts. I have volunteered with the Special Olympics, churches, and even ran a 5k for the American Heart Association. I also worked as a healthcare professional for 11 years and it was rewarding but the compensation was not there monetarily, but it was still liberating because it gave me the freedom to travel and learn the Spanish and Portuguese languages. Many people turn to professions that require a heart of giving back. If you want to be a social worker, a teacher, or a pastor; make sure your heart is giving and not for power or greed.

"The only way to pay back a friendship is to get in more debt"

— Forest Bynum

Date: 2016

Location: Direct Facebook Quote

Making friends on the college scene is fun, exciting, and also a part of networking in the community of fellow learners. Some friends are not close. Some friends become strategic allies in business. Some become your best man. In any aspect of friendship, how much is due for the acceptance of belonging?

It is said money can buy many things. It can by many tangible items. You can buy these items for the people you love. Certain things are not found on the store shelf or online store. These precious things can only be given away but have so much value. Friendship is one of these great possessions that you will cherish for the rest your life and eternity. I know the true friends I made in college still continue to last. I try to put my best efforts in retaining my friends and they are well worth the investment. The interest received is not from a mere loan but from dividends of respect and love.

I have found over the many years of my existence, that some friends are till the very end. No matter how much you do for them and vice versa, it will never be enough to satisfy the invoice of togetherness. So when a friend does you a favor, the best way to repay them is just to be there for them. You could be ministering to angels. Money can never buy friendship but just opportunities. I do not like the concept of fraternities and sororities except the fact they do great community service, because buying friends is a bad investment.

"Don't judge each day by the harvest you reap but by the seeds that you plant."

- Robert Louis Stevenson

Date: November 13, 1850 - December 3, 1894
Location: Unknown

Learning at the college level takes dedication and the ability to take pieces of knowledge from many places. To show what you learned, you must demonstrate that knowledge and sometimes repackage it to express your own thoughts. As you begin this journey, you will understand about the seasons of the semester or quarter and know when to plant and when to harvest.

Collecting knowledge is more than just attending class. Being observant of your surroundings helps. Learning how to use the resources of your library also can give you tools to collect facts for your studies. A good schedule can help study time be efficient. All these combined allow you to stand at the knowledge table and feast instead of just eat.

However, to truly obtain the information, you need to plant the seeds. The writing process is very important in expressing what you want to plant. Being able to perform on your test by adequate sleep and rest can help give back to your teachers that you have mastered the material. Planting the seeds of high marks will ensure another great harvest next semester or quarter. Your treasure island will await with completion of your degree. It is one thing to have access to eat from the harvest but better to plant the seeds for generations to come.

"I am not afraid of storms, for I am learning how to sail my ship."

- Louisa May Alcott

Date: November 29, 1832 - March 6, 1888

Location: Unknown

What an amazing person Louisa May Alcott turned out to be. She turned contracting typhoid fever while serving as a nurse in the American Civil War into a career of inspiring a nation of young people by her most famous historical recount of the time, <u>Little Women</u>. She continued to divulge into different genres of writing and lots of her writings are still distributed today.

Like many other famous artisans, she could transform the pain of typhoid fever which she battled for her lifetime into great literary works, a provider for her family, and a trendsetter for a changing country in its infancy of global society. Frida Kahlo also suffered many pains through her tragedies and transformed the art world of the 20th century. Both of these women not only had to navigate storms in their lives, but they also just had to live life.

In my life, I have to navigate storms. I am not famous but I deal with high blood pressure from stress and sometimes I get real sad because the loss of my immediate family. In college, just as in real life, you have to navigate storms. It is real tough sometimes especially without resources. I have learned that human resources are just as important as having money. You will find that issues will come as a college student, but those who are able to navigate the storms instead of give up or stay sheltered in the bay of mediocrity find themselves the captain of their destiny and accomplish the degree. When you finish your degree, you will still learn that you continue to learn how to run the ship.

"Woman must not depend upon the protection of man but must be taught to protect herself."

- Susan B. Anthony

Date: February 15, 1820 - March 13, 1906

Location: Unknown

When it comes to breaking new ground in academics and knowledge, college is the right place to be. However, many students don't make the big breakthrough but still contribute to learning and others may pick up where they left off. I am a big advocate of discovering new things while you are at these great institutions called universities. I hope that I am able to leave my legacy at my university.

Susan B. Anthony was more than a famous writer. She fought for rights for everyone. She was an abolitionist and help fight for the 14th amendment. She was most famous for her work in the suffrage movement. She traveled from state to state spreading the message that women needed to be able to vote. She did compelling work but was not able see the finish product after even the leader of the International Council of Women. Women received the right to vote 16 years after she passed away.

Great people like her do not get mention enough

in history as she set the standard for breaking new ground and being revolutionary. As you are working hard to gain the degree, remember that you might not see the finished product but your contribution can lead to greatness. By allowing women to vote, it has enriched our society and the overall quality of life. She did it to show women can stand on their own two feet. I challenge the ladies who read this book to not be afraid to protect yourself and dare to be bold in every academic endeavor. Your work might not make you a success but may lead other women to be stronger, wiser, and have a successful breakthrough.

"Facts are stubborn things, but statistics are pliable."

- Samuel Langhorne Clemens

Date: November 30, 1835 - April 21, 1910
Location: Unknown

Every true author can tell a good story. Sometimes the stories are true, sometimes the stories are false, and sometimes they can be false negatives, true positives, and the rare false, false, double negative. It is interesting that genius can show their brilliance in multiple areas. In your college career, you will run across many facts. Your textbooks will be filled with factual information you gather and be tested on including this double negative thing (I learned in Spanish you can actually speak in double negatives...in college) I learned about in grammar school.

Once a fact is established, outside of a new theory, it is accepted as fact. Statistics are a different story. Data is factual as long as it is conducted honestly by experimental procedure. When you study it, its results can rewrite the history of your opinion on a topic. A good politician can take data and convince you to vote for or against something based on manipulating the statistics.

Going to college you can learn a vide variety of

subjects, but I recommend that everyone take a statistics course. Learn about how to collect data, observe data, and read into the real results of data. By my knowledge of statistics, it helps me formulate opinions on every subject and understand the great mysteries of Fox News and The Price is Right. If you ever want to be a trendsetter, do research, or most graduate programs, you will need statistics.

"The activist is not the man who says the river is dirty. The activist is the man who cleans up the river"

- Ross Perot

Date: June 27, 1930 - Present

Location: Unknown

We all have great dreams to accomplish by going to college. We pursue our hopes and desires by taking advice and discovering wisdom on our own. Taking care of ourselves is important in the university life, but taking care of the external is a bit tricky sometimes. I see all the recycling bins around campus and wonder, "How much of that really gets used again?"

This moment in history tells the tale of a business owner that was confronted with a proposition to clean up a river solely because he had the money to do so. I learned about social responsibility and green marketing but it did not start to make sense till I saw the perspective of the businessman in question. He actually proposed to pay the protestor to clean it up. The protestor said that was not his job. Looks like we have a contradiction in beliefs.

So I think using our resources wisely is very important. I like to reuse containers instead of throwing them away. I save the sour cream and yogurt containers because they are 16 and 32 oz and make great Tupper-ware. My student worker job, we actually use the backs of all our prints unless it has sensitive information. Being responsible is more than saying we recycle, we actually have to do it. So do not just say you stand for something, be a participant. Voting is one way to show this principle. Another is to keep your appointments and promises. By doing this you will be trusted and people will be more willing to assist you to the goal of getting that degree.

"No es un barrio, es barrio mío"

- Forest D Bynum

Date: Dec 6, 2006

Location: San Telmo, Buenos Aires, Argentina

I went to Argentina in hopes for an unbelievable adventure and I was well rewarded as I hopped around South America for a few weeks and discovered a lot about life, a little about budgeting, and a tremendous mount about culture. One aspect I like about Latin American culture is the distinct flavor of neighborhoods in the major cities.

San Telmo is where I stayed in Buenos Aires and it was pretty neat just to walk around and see it on a street level. The graffiti, the cafes, the loud traffic; it is an incredible experience for someone who was a novice of the language. I saw many other neighborhoods like La Boca and Recoleta, but San Telmo will always have a special place in my heart. When I returned home, I read about the history and realized I was in the home of the Tango, one of the most iconic symbol of Argentina. I know it has its good, bad, and ugly roots, but I claim it as my home from home.

After my brief 18 year hiatus, I can see more of .

what I should have focused on but being part of the university is still needed. At LSU where sun dresses flow in the summer and the wisps of scantron and gridiron victories scent the air in the winter. It reminds me that it is my university. LSU is just not a place for school, but an institution that I hope will become legendary for my family and generations to come. So I do what I can to claim it my own. When you see yourself being involved on campus, life is more enjoyable, and you are more likely to chase pursuit of the degree.

"Nothing in life is to be feared, it is only to be understood. Now is the time to understand more, so that we may fear less."

- Marie Curie

Date: November 7, 1867 - July 4, 1934

Location: Unknown

This scientist shares with us so much more knowledge than just the radiation that comes from rocks. She gives us insight on how to approach learning and discovering ourselves. The older I get, the less I realize I know. That motivates me to want to learn more about everything. I was afraid to comeback to school for several years, but now that feeling is gone away.

For years I had the mindset of learning on my own and figuring things out by myself. It was tough, but it took myself of being stripped of almost nothing and sleeping on the sidewalk to not be afraid of going to college again. Four semesters later and I am still hungry to learn and discover more about business and researching at the university level. My senior classes are difficult but I embrace the challenge and you will too once you understand.

I also have to remember this principle when I try to be sociable and meet people. Meeting new people was a struggle for the first semester or two. Being a generation older made me out of place as I searched for a place to belong at the university. I try to smile and help people out when I can with the small things like opening doors and remembering to say thank you when people help me out. The fear of being social is more common than you think as SAD affect many college students. If you let fear overcome your understanding of networking and meeting people, check resources at your health and wellness center on campus.

"Equipped with his five senses, man explores the universe around him and calls the adventure Science."

- Edwin Powell Hubble

Date: November 20, 1889 - September 28, 1953
Location: Unknown

One of my favorite dishes is a tortilla. The sound of the olive oil popping from the pan as the potatoes place with precision. The smell of the green onions freshly chopped set aside to garnish. The dark yellow of the yolk knows my lady bought these eggs fresh. The brown edges come uniformly across knowing none stuck to the pan. The taste was so creamy but the seasoning balanced out the taste buds in my mouth. That is what I call observation.

Observation is a great tool as it starts the process of research and the whereabouts of your surroundings. Now imaging trying to observe an infinite universe like Mr. Hubble. I know about math and physics but that amount of symbols and squiggles he used in his studies warrants a keen eye to observing the heavens. It is so big, I just continue to wonder and ponder the big if's but realized that it is all contained in my Bible. I try to observe a little bit each day as my Bible seems to be infinite in knowledge, just like the cosmos that Edwin knew so well.

You can explore these observations as well. Seeing the stars is as easy as finding a spot without light pollution. Going to a website where you can see observations of his telescope. Taking an astronomy class and realizing that real astronomy is dealt through physics. Plus visiting a observatory can help you with observing the heavens. But observing goes further as most of you thought that tortilla was flat and made of corn or flour and that book is really, really good at observing the nature of yourself and humankind. Getting that degree would be easier with the art of observation.

"Actually, everything that can be known has a Number; for it is impossible to grasp anything with the mind or to recognize it without this."

- Philolaus

Date: 470 BC - 385 BC

Location: Ancient Greece

Pay attention in math class! Numbers are everything, but sometimes they can lie as they can be manipulated. Everything from recipes to research rely on numbers to back them up in college. Complaining about this will not help as eventually your pocketbook can dwindle if you do not understand how to balance it correctly. Be responsible of your bank account because I hate NSF fees, although it has been several years since I had one.

A number that is very important is the GPA. You will realize that you should do well early, often, and a strong finish. Your GPA determines a lot of your future including if you can take certain classes, get accepted to graduate school, or even get a job of your liking. I have been in operations management in the past and I would never hire anyone lower than a 3.0. This determines if you can live a good life or a great life. I had the uphill climb and was a 1.78 after one year, but now I am above a 3.0 and plan to stay there.

Numbers can do some many things in our live as

college students. They can be complex, as you figure out the flight path of a plane. They can be irrational, but useful like solving the interest in a security. Sometimes they are natural like the counting the syllables in your favorite poem. Numbers are powerful and are necessary in every curriculum, so pay attention in math class!

"At the end of the day it's not about what you have or even what you've accomplished… it's about who you've lifted up, who you've made better, it's about what you've given back."

- Denzel Washington

Date: December 28, 1954 - Present
Location: Unknown

It is a interesting comparison that two handsome black men made it in the movies, give great quotes about life, and flunked out their first year of college. The difference is that I was just an extra in a movie (I did make the final cut) that was shot on LSU's campus. The other things are true as well because I try to express myself with words of wisdom based on my experiences to make you better. I want to see others become better so I try to be encouraging to everyone, even those I do not know.

He obviously has a lot more than me as he has a list of films that stretches his diversity of acting to depths that I only can imagine. His accomplishments go beyond the silver screen but I have some achievements as well. It is more important that I give back what I know than the things I accomplish. And yes, we did both flunk our first year in college.

So as I encourage you to get that degree, I want you to give back what you know, some time to others in need, and money who really need it to survive. You should aspire to be little league coaches, tutors in your churches, and donate money and real food to people who are in need. It is one thing to earn the degree, good to make a living from your education, but great to be able to make someone's life better because of the diploma hanging from your wall. Don't be satisfied with just graduating, but put your life into good use.

"Carry your Green Book with you—You may need it"

- Victor Hugo Green

Date: November 9, 1892 - 1960

Location: Somewhere traveling the world

    As a fellow traveler, guidebooks are a great help. This quote really opened my eyes to US history and the influences in my life. This Green Book was created in 1936, during a time where black people were treated unfairly as they traveled. I have traveled the world and never have come across such discrimination. I learned so much from the international community.

    My travels are extensive as I dreamed of seeing the world and I was able to do so with the help of guidebooks. These books really helped defined my way of life as my favorite guidebook is <u>South America on a Shoestring</u>. From using these guides, I became proficient in the way of the backpacker and have become a travel expert myself. You really have to strap on the shoestrings of someone else's boot before you know how they truly live.

    When I first started college, I had a bad experience as I was told by several people of my race that you should only speak with African-Americans. 50 years ago this may have been the case as the author had experienced the same trials as my father had with racism when he was young. To survive in college, you must be able to see beyond the color of one's skin. Appreciate what others bring in discussions and in research. There is no such guide to help you navigate the injustices of ignorance. This goes beyond race; also free yourself from discrimination against international students and gender. Don't stick to your own kind.

"Administration is my job, travel is my university"

- Forest D. Bynum

Date: February 2014

Location: Haven Church

 I had just published my second book in one of the coldest winters recorded in Louisiana history. It was also cold in my heart as it started to settle in I would never find work again. The walls of the church started to close in as I saw bars of overqualified skill put me in a prison I couldn't escape. The building was dilapidated and the chill was overcome by the stench of ineptitude of my experiences before becoming homeless. I was determined to find work instead of falling into the trap of government reliance.

 I realize 27 months without full time work would have been a great opportunity to complete most of my coursework at university, but I felt that I truly should be in the workforce. I knew I was great at administration, but even the simplest of vocation would not let me break me from the cycle of despair in my heart. I had interview, but only for the professional positions and some even required a degree.

 I finally got into full time work again and I was given a pink slip 6 months later. This time I was able to actually secure a job so I had a little break. I fulfilled a promised that I would travel to Spain again someday and surprised everyone. Everyone was upset with me but they have to realize, no one wanted me to leave the church to my own apartment. I had the money for I had saved several thousands of dollars, but I kept getting denied for apartment applications.

I knew then my hashtag was true that I motivated myself with during the hateful process. I knew administration was just a job, but I learned through my travels. That is why I decided when I was kicked out of the church when I was fired that I was going to pursue jobs that I wanted to do and not just for the money. I finally was pushed on the streets and I decided on going back to school for something I truly wanted to learn and discover. My degree will allow me to become an international businessperson. When you declare your major, don't trap yourself in a prison, do something that you love.

"This conflict is one thing I've been waiting for. I'm well and strong and young - young enough to go to the front. If I can't be a soldier, I'll help soldiers."

- Clara Barton

Date: December 25, 1821 - April 12, 1912

Location: Unknown

I have been a supporter of the armed forces my whole life, but I do not necessarily like the idea of war. When my father was young, he fought in WWII in the Navy. He taught me some of the things he learned but I did not know his whole story. I knew he tried to go to college, but he never graduated. I understand the threat of WWII and the reason why he would serve.

So I celebrate the soldiers whenever I can. I like to sit in the Memorial Oak Grove and remember those who fought so I can go to college. I enjoy hearing the stories of veterans. The fireworks of the Fourth of July. Reach out to those wounded in battle; they go through real battles we do not understand.

There are many battles we fight at college. They are not as severe as holding off the threats of dictators, but they are important to us as we are in these trenches of life looking for a way to win the campaign. Some of us don't fight these battles, but we see our fellow students on these battlefronts. We are not generals but we can take the same role as Clara Barton did and saved lives by helping. We can't take each others tests or do others homework, but or best role is to help. We need to spot out wounded soldiers and bring them to the tent to get healed. Whether it is tutoring, family issues, or drug addiction; we may not be equipped to fight but help through the cross. If you see someone slipping, help them to complete the degree, because that person was me.

"Travel is fatal to prejudice."

- Mark Twain

Date: November 30, 1835 - April 21, 1910
Location: Unknown

    I learned to fight racism through learning about other cultures. Before college, I was not exposed to many cultures. It was the way I grew up. I had read about them, but I did not interact with a lot of people. I took three years of Spanish in high school because I wanted to go to Spain one day. I never imagined I would go three times and want to go again for Study Abroad for a least a semester, if not a year.

    When I first stepped into the hallowed halls of LSU, it was a new experience for me socially. I could talk to people and actually get to know them personally. I had never eaten at a Chinese restaurant until I went to college. I still remember the sting of the horseradish in the yellow mustard as one of my dear friends said it was delicious. It was incredible spicy but I learned that day that I shouldn't eat what I grew up with but taste culture. From there I did mission work in Mexico, did a tour in South America, visited India, backpacked my way through Europe, and got to see a friend's homeland in the Dominican

Republic.

My most memorable culture shock was my first visit to Spain. When I decided to go back to college, this was one of the things I considered. It was a unforgettable experience when I entered the Plaza Mayor and saw all the people. Everything was so different but I immersed myself right away. It was more than the Museo del Prado or the Museo de Jamon. It was the way they talked, they played, they ate, they lived. I fell in love and I knew at that point I wanted travel to be part of my life. This is why I work so hard in college, so I can have this experience over and over again. Learn other cultures…it is a good thing.

"Reading brings us unknown friends"

- Honoré de Balzac

Date: May 20, 1799 - August 18, 1850

Location:

     When I was small, I was an avid reader. I was frequent at the library reading all the books in sight especially the world geography section. I would read old textbooks and anything that dealt with non-fiction. It all stopped in 6th grade when reading no longer became fun. I realized the social isolation and it took me a couple of years that I needed to force myself to be a lot more outgoing in order to be part of people's lives.

     It was not until college I truly realized the importance of reading. Being able to comprehend text is vital in the academic setting of any major. They use reading comprehension as a measurement of how well you can learn. My ability to comprehend actually went down as I entered LSU and may have hurt me when I first started out. I did not pick up reading again till I started traveling and I read the classics for fun. I learned of the exciting tales of yesteryear and I went on a trip from Istanbul to Paris inspired by the book <u>Murder on the Orient Express</u>.

Now I started back and I love to read. I read the newspaper and articles on <u>The Wall Street Journal</u>. I have to read a lot for my classes and I have started to read some of the Spanish classics. My comprehension has come back for the most part and I get to know parts of history and culture through many of the new characters in the books. I do not advise spending all your time reading. Take a look in a book sometime, you may find a <u>Reading Rainbow</u> as you will be like the butterfly in the sky that makes you fly twice as high. Also, it will help you to understand the material in class and get you one step closer to obtaining the degree.

"What is a soul? It's like electricity - we don't really know what it is, but it's a force that can light a room. "

- Ray Charles

Date: September 23, 1930 - June 10, 2004
Location: Unknown

On December 2008, I had Georgia on My Mind as I was set on my midnight bus to Atlanta. I experienced the soul of Southern cooking and got to visit many places including my favorite restaurant, Fogo de Chão. When I search deeper within myself on this outings during Christmas time, I realize that I runaway from the fact of not having my biological family to celebrate with. I spent a few Christmases with a couple of my dear friends, but it is not the best of holidays for me.

A deep part of my soul that is a bit dark but flavorful with memories is my yearly ritual of glasses of rum while listening to Rhythm and Blues on Christmas Day. The darker the better as I seek out libations from my travels or make visits with Mr. Meyers and Ms. Bacardi. I may have three or four drinks on Christmas and a couple on Boxing Day, but it may not be the best was to celebrate the birth of my savior.

When pursuing the college degree, it is so much more than academics. You should pour your soul into your studies, but not forget the people you are closest to. I have done some great things in the past to celebrate Christmas but there is bit of an empty void without my dear friends. I was in Brazil one year, Argentina one year, Spain in another; yet I was able to learn but not truly satisfy the soul till I came home. Do not be so consumed in your studies you forget to satisfy your soul. It can truly light up a room when you meet friends and family. I am having to correct this mistake by writing time off on my schedule for friends.

"The more I read, the more I acquire, the more certain I am that I know nothing."

- Voltaire

Date: November 21, 1694 - May 30, 1778

Location: Paris, France

I am 38 years young and still am computing the value of education. My Calculus class in high school was probably the biggest investment in my education of all time. It gives me the ability to problem solve anything. Reading is important as well. Thinking all the way back to ancient times where most traditions were oral unless things like laws and trade were being recorded by the governments and court of the day. Reading was such a privilege and until the time of Christ, only members of high society could have access to writing. Somehow, the New Testament has the most copies of any book written before the printing press. Makes you think twice of the impact of Christianity.

During Medieval Times, when the hand of the Roman Empire was lifted off of Western Europe, society decayed there while other cultures grew and thrive due to the production of books. Let us not forget the empires of Timbuktu and Constantinople. Books were prevalent as even with Charlemagne and some of the Catholic churches cherished books just as much as jewels or precious metals.

As we progressed into the years of history and books became more accessible, the access to higher learning was available to more people. This allowed for narrower topics to be studied and more specialties in the job market. With technology bringing us to a new age of learning, I understand that as I get more access to knowledge, the less I really know. It reminds me of the history foretold by these great scholars and writers before me. So when you finish your degree, realizes the learning has just begun. New information will arise and new books will be written which I will want to read.

"Embrace the old, experience the new."

- Roksaburo Michibia

Date: January 3, 1931 - Present

Location: Kitchen Stadium

If memory serves me correctly, 19 years ago I started my culinary battle career. I was challenged by a former roommate that he could make fudge better than I could. I was in the beginnings of learning about cooking as I used recipes from the red Betty Crocker bible (a cookbook my friend let me use that was developed in the 1960's) and I loved the candy making section because of the chemistry involved in the process. He even made the preposterous statement that his grandfather invented the Kraft recipe on the jar of marshmallow crème. My fudge won and I had future battles which I had a cookie duel, the 24 hour pork battle, the solanaceous fruit battle, and the Battle Royal of King Cake. I learned to use new information from watching Food Network but still have that red Bible from generations ago.

From the wisdom of the wise sage I also was discovering my faith and Christ Jesus and came with the same conclusion that we lived in the New Testament but we had to learn from the Old Testament in order to experience the full grace of Jesus. The disciples did not have the privilege of the New Testament, they used the Old Testament to reach believers, giving it validity today. The Jews in the text gave wisdoms and great stories of faith as it described in Hebrews 13. I had to realize after my baptism I needed to spend time studying the Old Testament as well as daily reading of the New Testament. I met with a group of Messianic Jews and I discovered they used a lot of the Old Testament in the two hour service. They were great as I learned a lot of Torah, balance a yamaka on my stylish fro, and learned the art of nosh. It was very similar to eating tapas, which you know I enjoy very much.

This lesson came again as I went back to school. I enjoyed doing research and the smell of the new notebook, but you really have to know how to use a computer. I did an entire research paper with using archives on the Internet by the university library system. I did not check out one book that semester. Most of my textbooks are electronic. I speak to my professors with my smartphone by e-mail, as when 20 years ago, you had to visit their office. You still need to study hard and a pencil with paper still does wonders for taking notes. My economics professor gave our class a study on note taking and students that use paper and pencil did significantly better than those who used their laptop to take notes. I once again had to understand in order to get my degree, I had to embrace the old but experience the new.

"Great things are done by a series of small things brought together."

- Vincent Van Gogh

Date: March 30, 1853 - July 29, 1890

Location: Unknown

The most famous work of Van Gogh was the Starry Night. His post impressionistic style allowed him to create a series of techniques to make this beautiful masterpiece. Being this skillful, you have to be able to use several small techniques to bring worthiness to the canvas. He had to learn about how to use colors, perspective, and sketching before he could really start doing the numerous still-life's and landscapes he created.

When I first learned how to cook, I did it by learning recipes but I eventually learned small techniques. I learned how to boil, poach, stir fry, and grill. I learned the basics of baking and using yeast and making quick breads, candy, and cakes. It took me a few years to start scribbling recipe ideas and 2007 I started creating original recipes. Five years later, I published my first cookbook.

In order to complete your degree, you must learn the small techniques in order to achieve your masterpiece. By using study skills, algebraic methods, and time management; you can move on to the bigger tasks later in your curriculum. Without mastering the smaller tasks, you just memorize a bunch of stuff, forget it, and then go back to sleep. Your time in college will be of "what can I do to finish" instead of "what can I build upon for the future". Vincent painted that painted at the end of his life after he cut his ear off. It was in the asylum that he displayed his masterful ways of the brush. I know this same feeling as my time in the asylum in November 2018 I created a picture of Latin American Fruits using a sheet of paper and broken crayons. There were no fruits to be spoken of in the facility to eat or to be inspired.

" There is a cost for every decision we make and a value for those decisions we don't make. "

- Forest Bynum

Date: Unknown

Location: Unknown

In the era of online investment companies and alternative currencies like Bitcoin and the Petro, getting money is more than running a paper route or working part time as a bag boy at your local grocery store. Learning how to deal with money is a paramount pursuit you must tackle if you want to reach the summit of graduation. Everything has a cost, even the things you do not purchase. If you look at the cost as the value being used up to perhaps do or purchase something else, then you have stumbled upon a primary principle of economics called opportunity cost.

In college, you can spend your money easily and I warn you to pay close attention to how you spend your greenbacks. Budgeting will allow you to weigh the necessary decisions on your level of purchase power and determine the way you live. If you are not good with money, I would suggest you find someone to sit you down and help you keep track of it and to make sound purchases. But in college, time is just as valuable as money.

Say you have an hour, you can spend that hour studying, playing video games, resting, sleeping, working, or talking with friends. Making a schedule is also as valuable as learning how to keep track with your money. Time has a cost and it also has value. Opportunities come and go and while you are here, sometimes you need to have fun, sometimes study, and sometimes rest. You can always make more money, but you can't get time back.

"What moves men of genius, or rather what inspires their work, is not new ideas, but their obsession with the idea that what has already been said is still not enough."

- Eugene Delacroix

Date: April 26, 1798 - August 13, 1863

Location: Unknown

It is my culinary passion that brought me to discover this influential 19th century artist. They call Iron Chef Japanese II, Hiroyuki Sakai, the Delacroix of Cuisine. I read that Delacroix was noted for his use of color and the ability of knowing optics he could easily differentiate shades in his artwork and lithography. He also inspired other famous artists like Vincent Van Gogh, Pablo Picasso, and Pierre Renoir.

I am deeply involved with my pursuit of the undergraduate degree. I love business and I enjoy learning how it affects the world. I no longer have the longings to become a chef, but want to do better as a cookbook writer. I want to write a second edition of my cookbook someday and I want to explore into writing a series of other cookbooks I have started. It is one thing to come up with ideas, but to build upon them for greater works is very difficult especially when life gets in the way of carrying out these grandiose hobbies of mine.

I have learned from my experiences in college that

it is not good enough to have ideas. When I was writing my research paper for my English class, I knew I did not want to write about exactly as the teacher gave us general topics, but transform the category into something I knew about and that I could add my own ideas to in order to achieve success. I know of several people that said they can write a book, teach a class, or start a business. It takes effort, time, some money, and you need to improve on what you have done before. You need to show what you learned, even on the smallest of scales. You need to seek to pursue your own ideas and build upon what is taught. This will help you with the struggle to graduate.

"It is not easy to be a pioneer - but oh, it is fascinating!"

- Elizabeth Blackwell

Date: February 3, 1821 - May 31, 1910

Location: Unknown

    I never had the inkling to pursue a degree in the medical field. With my knowledge in healthcare administration, several people requested me to go back to school to be a nurse. I know a few nurses as they are my dear friends and I just do not have the type of compassion needed to be a nurse. I know my arenas; business, food, travel, Spanish, and making tasty sandwiches. She was the first woman ever to obtain a medical degree in the United States. She never set out to be a pioneer, her hard work propelled her to become one as she became a physician back in her country in England.

    A few people I know tried the pre med route. They were good students but realized their best skills were in other arenas. That is one thing I give to my friends; they used their skills and committed to their craft. So while I sat in the depths of depression dishing out doughnuts for mere duckets of despair; they became an accountant, lawyer, IT specialist, and a geographer.

    So I want to encourage all of those who want to be

the future doctors, dentists, and nurse practitioners of the world. You need to stay on your grind and learn everything. Take summer school every semester and you need to shoot for an 4.0 to be competitive. Speak with your financial aid office every year to find more scholarship money, you will need it as the classes are designed to weed out the good, mediocre, and the bad. Remember, you will be competing not only with each other but also pure science students and engineers for the couple A's given out in each section. Because when you finally become a doctor, you need to make friends with a financier you an trust to invest your money, you are going to need it, it is called malpractice, and lots of unscrupulous people will take your heard earned money after 12 or 15 years of school and practicums.

"A society must assume that it is stable, but the artist must know, and must let us know, that there is nothing stable under heaven."

- James Baldwin

Date: August 2, 1924 - December 1, 1987

Location: Unknown

We can assume that in the United States as of 2019 we have a stable economy, a stable currency, and not very much social uprising. James Baldwin was able to experience a life in pre and post civil rights America and he was able to share his views and rubbed shoulders with famous people in every circle. He knew Langston Hughes, Sidney Poitier, and even Ray Charles. He was known for standing up for what he believed in and lived a good portion of his life in France. As a writer, he approached topics such as racism, sexuality freedom, and social injustice.

I do not necessarily agree with all the viewpoints of Mr. Baldwin nor do I choose to judge his life for knowing what my father went through, I probably would have made the decision to either fight or leave for my protection. He was exposed to WWII, the Korean War and the Vietnam Conflict. He was also part of shaping the African-American culture even while living abroad. He was a great writer and poet and his statement is true that an artist needs to be ready to take criticism from everyone. His expression was not liked by everyone but only could be guaranteed to be accepted by the LORD.

Over the years I have learned that art is subjective. For those who are art majors, you will need to embrace yourself that your paintings alone may not support you after you get your degree. I always encourage my friends who want to pursue art to learn the business side to make it a living. Very few artists live off of their work alone and it requires several years of teaching, dedication, and mastering of technique. I encourage the arts because it inspires us all, but be ready for criticism, most people may like your work to be nice but not nice enough to pay you for your hard work.

"If they don't give you a seat at the table, bring a folding chair."

- Shirley Chisholm

Date: January 1969

Location: in the U.S. Congress

Of all the influential African Americans discussed in this book, she is one of the most note worthy. She was the first black woman ever to be elected to Congress. Her work in the Civil Rights movement gave her the opportunity to reach out to her district and was voted in to express the inequality in American society. You would think someone would be defeated when she was not treated the same, but she would make her own statement and also be the first black woman to make a major run at the Presidency in 1972.

If you believe in something, you have to make a statement. She made an impact with American families by helping the WIC program to start and also that the government to help pay for child care for women to enter the workplace. I made my first statement by help funding a mission trip in 2000. I raised money by selling baked goods in front of Wal-Mart. I saved money from my job. I took three weeks off to ride through the Coahuila desert to deliver toys and a bike to an orphanage. I helped build a wall at a church, taught vacation Bible School, and sang in the choir...all in Spanish. I was not always accepted at church and still look for a church home since I was homeless.

If you feel you are discriminated in any way, in most cases, there are ways to fight back. You can complain but complaining will just protect you from getting hurt, it does not advance the situation or bring justice to the situation in question. As she still faced discrimination during her long tenure on Capitol Hill, she made her own way to accomplish her goals. To make strides to getting the degree, you need to be ready to learn at any cost. You may not be invited to that study session. They may not allow you to take that job unless you make a way to show you are qualified. My advice is to be ready to be kind, think outside the box, and work harder than anyone else...by working diligently and smarter.

"Eratosthenes, the mapmaker who was the first man to accurately measure the size of the Earth, was a librarian."

- Ken Jennings

Date: May 23, 1974 - Present

Location: Unknown

The famous philosophers back in ancient times were taught in all sorts of things. They knew many subjects because universities back then were just hubs of wisdom. They did not take classes or have degree audits. They just listed, observed, performed calculations, and experiments to show what they knew. Yes, Eratosthenes was these things and the chief librarian of one of the Seven Wonders of the World, the Library of Alexandria. To just call him a librarian is an understatement. Ken Jennings is known for recalling these odd facts from memory for money and now writes children's books.

Both of these men exemplify the great uses of education to become great men in their day. Learning in a higher institution, the great students do learn many disciplines although modern universities continue to make degrees more specific. Take advantage of the university arena and learn everything well. I know that some courses you may think are in the way but you will never know when you need to draw a map or help someone find a good book. These are honorable professions like writing children's stories and being a computer scientist. So as you focus on completing your degree, I stress the importance of options. Find out what you can do with your degree, you may be surprised in what roads you can take.

"Once a man stops his learning, he starts to die"

- Forest Bynum

Date: 2015

Location: Haven Church

I have endured many of rough times where I though life was not needed to be completed anymore. I have been without friends, family, food, and just trust in humankind. I have been through sadness, depression, and anxiety of when I would have purpose again. There are a few things I have not ever lost, hope in Christ, faith in my skills, and the yearning to learn.

Learning takes on so many facets in your life. Anytime you read something, watch something, add numbers, or complete an action; learning takes place. If you sit idle, you will start to decay. As I sat in a building of neglect, I had to encourage myself by reading anything I could find, listening to anything of redeeming value, and using my creativity to keep my mind active.

To obtain your degree, you need to be continuously learning. If you have to take a break, make it as small as possible. Do not wait to finish your degree, finish while you are young. I tell you from experience that it can be done at a later life, but prejudices will follow. Somehow scholarships are hard to find when you are 38 and make the Dean's List multiple times. You will find most people and employers will rush you to get any degree instead what you want to learn. For those who want to major in a foreign language, you will need to practice over the breaks to stay at your fluency level and grow. When you finish your degree, keep learning, find something to do for one hour a week that stimulates the mind. By doing this you will promote better mental and physical health. When I was removed from college, I almost started to die, but then I started my first shift as a line cook at Louie's Café. The choose your own adventure of my life truly began.

Epilogue:

The Fall of 2017 brought in a crisp air of new job skills. I learned about invoices and what an accountant goes through. Miss Candy was a great boss. She trusted me to do the real calculations under her careful eye and exposed me to the necessary evil of paying the bills. She was so friendly and knew pretty much every vendor and department by name. I learned a lot from her as she gave me great study techniques and showed me the real side of accounting. My new home made my new school schedule possible. My Spanish teacher did not have enough students to teach me the next level of Spanish, so I received permission to take SPAN 2101 at LSU while enrolled at the community college. I was a few minutes from LSU from my apartment but an hour commute from the community college. I made the trek from 6AM till 5PM Monday thru Friday and never missed a class except for one Biology class. It was tough, but I also worked twenty hours a week in Accounts Payable till Finals week. I had no furniture to speak of and I still do not have any to this day. I manage to do homework with a folding table and a chair I bought at a second-hand store. I did Biology projects, recorded speeches, did countless hours of accounting homework, practice writing Spanish, but was moved by MATH 2303.

My statistics class was also very memorable as I had taken AP Statistics in high school but this time I would be taught by someone who really understood the study of data. My statistics professor had an uncanny approach to teaching by making sure we could work examples in class and she would challenge us by being tough in the material but always being available for help. Believe it or not, it was the theory I asked for help, the arithmetic was second nature. During the semester, I saw a fellow classmate in my Accounting class had forgot his calculator and look worried. My intuition kicked in and I asked my statistics professor if I could borrow her calculator for the test. She said yes, and I forever had the utmost respect for her. Through this transaction, I met my friend and brother Nicholas. I let him use the calculator and we became study partners. We lived life and shared laughs and tears. We would wind up getting good grades in Accounting through our shared efforts. Now all was left was the Statistics final.

I had a 97 going into the Final. I was studying a chapter a day until a snowstorm came into Baton Rouge. This was the first time in over 15 years the snow would stick to the ground. The community college wanted to cancel exams and they did, but my professor does not know of the kind act she did that semester. She gave us the opportunity to take the final early before the snowstorm hit. I was saving my money from my job to go to learn more Spanish in the Dominican Republic. I decided to take my final early. I probably received an A on the final, but I got an 80 which allowed to secure an A. If I would not have been able to take the final early, I would have missed my flight and not been able to go to the Dominican Republic.

As I was adjusting to my new abode, I picked up a new writing project. I was going to write a publication in Spanish. I wanted the challenge and it was tough as I did not know how to edit for grammar very well. I also was writing late at night and as early as 3 or 4 in the morning. I took an oral examination in my Spanish class and got the idea as I spouted of the vocabulary I learned from my teacher. I decided to just write about a new culinary experience but it turned into a learning exercise about learning adjectives which I still hope to write one day, so I can't divulge my secrets in this story. I decided to go to the DR to get research for the book. I planned everything and wrote an income statement to show I would have plenty of money to discover how people lived in Santo Domingo. Once again, I was pressured by discrimination by several people, but I had a secret. I met with a longtime friend of mine that was a former LSU student who I kept in touch with. He made my experience wonderful as I got to eat an authentic Christmas Caribbean meal and went camping with him. I got to eat lunch with his family and had wonderful discussions in Spanish about life, laughter, and friendship. I would abandon the writing project due to the discrimination but learned that Spanish needed to be part of my future. I declared my Spanish minor at the end of the semester.

When I came back, I had made straight A's again and was conditionally accepted into LSU. The Spring brought new challenged as I learned about data analytics, money and banking, and how hard it is for a 37-year-old to find part time work. I managed to find work on campus at International Studies. Being able to help the international community allowed me to give back to all the adventures and people I learned so much from. I was doing very well in all my classes except economics. I learned a very important lesson in learning, being able to accept you don't understand something. I got a C- on my first test after a generous curve and I was upset. I went to every class and I studied. I took advantage of the Center of Academic Success after the advice of my Economics teacher. It worked. I learned a better strategy of studying and I was able to get a B in the course. I was able to get a 3.8 that semester and knew I belonged at university. If only my neighbors approved of this same sentiment?

I had problems with noise and interruptions that would spell disaster in the near future. I felt alone as I was on an island by myself. I did not see others in my apartment complex with textbooks or bookbags. They were not respectful of my school schedule or college life. I thought I had moved into a student residence. It was just another place to live, but at least it was better than the inn.

Summertime approached, and I continued to work for International Studies. On my own time I would explore everything except the swimming pool. I was determined to keep focused on school. I kept reviewing Spanish by watching YouTube clips. I also tried out Python and Natural Talk Language for an idea I had to write a text writer for the Catalan language. I took a class online sponsored by the Generalitat in Catalonia and completed the A levels. I researched how I could continue my love of Statistics in business and ran across Econometrics. I read a few textbooks I downloaded and realized the potential it could have in my life. My future was coming together as I was determined to push myself and get the most out of my degree. It was a lonely time as I would reminisce the days of young as the Fresh Prince of Bel Air would use summertime to show off his fly ride. I would be babysat by the public library. Chris Bridges would drop his hotlanta hits and I was stuck in the drudgery between minimum wage and the living wage. My journey was halfway done as I was a Junior now, but it was lacking emotional support and fun from my dear friends.

On August of 2018, I embarked on one of the hardest school schedules my classmates say they had ever heard of being attempted. I was taking six classes including two ECON classes of a graduate level. I was told later that I took them out of sequence but was determined to finish my concentration of Empirical Analysis, so

I could do undergraduate research. My health suffered as I went through sleep deprivation through the problems of my apartment complex. I tried to handle the situation, but I had called the cops on February 2017 and they told me I would be committed to a psych ward if I called the police again. I was suspicious of discrimination again which is a part of being African-American. You try not to take the bitter sting of racism to heart, but I knew something was not right about the demeanor of the supposed public servant. So, I lived with the noise and the constant caterwauling of complaints of neighbors that did not like my alarm going off early in the morning or the waves of soft jazz or reggaetón during the day.

I also suffered through a misdiagnosis because I took the advice of my boss and went to get help with an advocacy group. They advised counseling that turned into discouragement and a self-image problem that stagnated my ability of learning. I reported of the many issues of my apartment and had to find private counseling away from the university to regain my composure of life. I spiraled into a debt of lost assignments and missed classes, and all was almost lost for the semester. I had a hospital stay where I was held against my will for ten days for I thought at the time was hypertension. I have dealt with hypertension for three years at that point and it was inconvenient, but it did not stop me from work or school. I kept my hope in the fact that I was going to finish my degree and I had unfinished business. I finally was let out the hospital and spent an extra two weeks to catch up my work for the semester. During that hospital stay of inadequate food, no heater, and lack of support; I concluded I needed to go all in my education. I decided to pursue a double major in Spanish and International trade and Finance, no matter how long it would take. I also decided to concentrate my

Spanish degree on Linguistics because I loved learning foreign languages and it would be handy to use my business research techniques to explore more of the field.

Now I am a Senior at Louisiana State University, a little more than a year removed from sleeping on a bus bench off Acadian Thurway. I look forward to another full schedule of advanced grammar in Spanish and lots of Economics. I am concentrating all my learning in the hopes to do research the last couple of semesters of my undergrad degrees. I am going to pursue the possibilities of learning Portuguese and Galician through Study Abroad through the proceeds of this book. My faith has never wavered, but I still have not been able to find a church home. I am so busy learning that I have neglected the time to find that place of worship. But I have learned through this chapter in life that I have not found the treasure chest of redemption. I want to graduate in the dual degree program with two degrees simultaneously. I dedicate my business degree to my father who never got to finish his degree, he fought for our country in WWII. I dedicate my Spanish degree for myself to prove that my traveling was not in vain, as I invested my life savings learning about the Hispanoamerica world. It was just God's way of directing my career. I hope when I graduate to pursue a career in Econometrics overseas or to become a Spanish teacher at the university level. These are the wise sayings of men and women that have shaped my passion for learning and I hope you find the path of academic righteousness to the promise land of graduation day.